Clever Girl Finance

Clever Girl Finance

Expanded and Updated

Ditch Debt, Save Money, and Build Real Wealth

Bola Sokunbi

WILEY

Published by John Wiley & Sons, Inc., Hoboken, New Jersey.
Published simultaneously in Canada.

For general information on our other products and services or for technical support, please contact our Customer Care Department within the United States at (800) 762-2974, outside the United States at (317) 572-3993 or fax (317) 572-4002.

Wiley also publishes its books in a variety of electronic formats. Some content that appears in print may not be available in electronic formats. For more information about Wiley products, visit our web site at www.wiley.com.

Library of Congress Cataloging-in-Publication Data is Available:

ISBN 9781394266944 (Paperback)
ISBN 9781394266968 (ePub)
ISBN 9781394266951 (ePDF)

Cover Design: Wiley
Cover Image: Courtesy of Clever Girl Finance

SKY10086339_100124

This book is dedicated to the original clever girl,
my incredible mother, Emily, and to all the clever girls who
have chosen to take ownership of their financial futures
and make their dreams come true.

Contents

About the Author xi

Also by Bola Sokunbi xiii

Acknowledgments xv

Welcome to the Expanded and Updated Edition of This Book! xvii

You Are in the Right Place xix

How to Use This Book xxi

Introduction xxiii

My Story xxxi

Part I The Start 1

Your *What* and Your *Why* 3

Chapter 1 Your Mindset 11

Let Go of Your Money Mistakes 13
Becoming Emotionally Balanced for a Positive Money Mindset 18
Meet Dr. Chavonne Perotte 23
Dream Big: Affirm Yourself to Being Wealthy 27
Shift Your Circle of Influence 32
Meet Latoya Scott 37

Chapter 2 Get Organized 41

Get Your Records In Order 43
Track Your Spending 50
Identify Your Bad Money Habits 55

Meet Christina Mychas 61
Know Your Net Worth 67
Meet Brittney Suttle 70
Define Your Values 73
Set Your Goals 75
Meet Molly Stillman 78

Part II The Plan 81

Chapter 3 Budgeting 83
Budgeting 101: The Basics 85
Setting Up Your Budget Using Categories 87
Budgeting Styles 90
Don't Ignore Your Money Leaks 96
Common Budgeting Challenges and How to Get Out of Your Own Way 100
Rewarding Yourself 102
Meet Esther Bangura 106
Budgeting on an Inconsistent Income 111
Budgeting on a Low Income 113
Budgeting as a Couple 115
The Save Yourself Fund: Your Emergency Savings 121
Sinking Funds to Stay on Track 124
My Story: How I Saved over $100,000 in Three Years 126

Chapter 4 Debt and Loans 131
Let's Talk About Debt. . .Because It Sucks 133
Paying Off Your Debt 139
Student Loans: Facts and Basics 145
Meet Melisa Boutin 146
Where to Start with Your Student Loans 148
Ideas to Pay Off Your Debt Fast 155
Meet Naseema McElroy 160
Cashback and Rewards Credit Cards 162
Meet Monica Louie 164

Chapter 5 Investing 171
Investing 101 173
Meet Adeola Omole 182
Investing for Retirement 185

How to Start Investing 192
Meet Mabel Nunez 197

Part III The Necessary 203

Chapter 6 Credit 205
Credit 101 207
Credit Scores 209
Busting Credit Myths 218
Compromised Information 221
Meet Rosemary A.B. 223

Chapter 7 Protecting Yourself 229
Creating a Backup Plan with the Right Insurance 231
Recession-Proofing Your Finances 239
Meet Ashlee Sang 247

Chapter 8 Making More Money 251
Negotiating to Win 253
Meet Steph May 259
Side Hustles 266
Meet Lucille Roache 271

Chapter 9 Your Self-Care 277
Nuturing Your Self-Care Alongside Your Financial Wellness. . .Because Yes 279

Chapter 10 Key Financial Actions 285
Steps to Keep Your Financial Plans Intact 286
In Closing 291

Appendix 293
Index 297

About the Author

Bola Sokunbi is a Certified Financial Education Instructor (CFEI), investor, finance expert, speaker, podcaster, bestselling author, and the founder and CEO of Clever Girl Finance, one of the largest personal finance media/education platforms for women in the U.S.

She is the recipient of the 2021 Financial Education Instructor of the Year (FEIY) Award from the National Council of Financial Educators (NFEC). Clever Girl Finance has also earned the Distinguished Personal Finance Content (DPFC) designation from the National Financial Educators Council, having proven competency in providing financial education that aligns with industry best practices and research-based education principles.

Based on Bola's experience saving over $100,000 in three and a half years after graduating from college and navigating through various financial mistakes and successes of her own in the years that followed, Bola started Clever Girl Finance in 2015 to provide women with the tools and resources she wished she had when she began her financial journey.

She lives with her husband and twins in New Jersey.

Also by Bola Sokunbi

My Wealth Plan: A Workbook by Clever Girl Finance

Learn How Investing Works, Grow Your Money

The Side Hustle Guide: Build a Successful Side Hustle and Increase Your Income

Choosing to Prosper: Triumphing Over Adversity, Breaking Out of Comfort Zones, Achieving Your Life and Money Dreams

Acknowledgments

This book would not be possible without the support and encouragement of some amazing people in my life.

To my parents, Tunji and Emily, for instilling the important money and life lessons that have helped me grow into the woman and mother I am today.

To my husband, Gbolabo, for being my number-one fan, motivator, and super-dad from the very beginning of the idea for Clever Girl Finance.

To my twins, Ore and Jola, my most precious gifts. I have grown so much being your mother, and I'm so proud of who you are each becoming. I am forever grateful for all the joy you bring to my life.

To all my incredible friends, family, and mentors, who have encouraged me through the ups and downs of growing Clever Girl Finance while balancing life at the same time – I am so grateful to have you in my life.

To my business advisors, Dan and Amy Stoller, Monique Nelson, Roshi Givechi, Jonathan Cornelissen, and Maureen Jules-Perez, for all your support and counsel, and for believing in me and my big vision.

To the entire Techstars family, for the incredible opportunity to join the ranks of Techstars companies and for providing me with the platform, resources, and mentorship to build a highly successful company.

To the incredible Clever Girl Finance team, for your endless support and dedication to making this book and our platform overall a success.

To the amazing women whose stories and advice are featured throughout this book, thank you so much for being a part of this journey.

To my book publisher, Wiley, and my supporting book editors, thank you for the opportunity to get this book out into the world.

To the Clever Girl Finance Tribe and to everyone who has supported and shared my message and mission, I would not be here today without you. I appreciate you more than words can express. I am honored and humbled to be able to positively impact your financial journey.

Thank you so much for everything!

Bola

Welcome to the Expanded and Updated Edition of This Book!

Welcome to this expanded and updated edition of *Clever Girl Finance: Ditch Debt, Save Money, and Build Real Wealth*! Whether you are a new or returning reader, thank you so much for picking up a copy.

I can't believe it's been six years since I wrote the first edition of this book. When this book was first released in 2019, I couldn't have imagined the tumultuous ride the world was about to take. From grappling with an unexpected global pandemic to navigating through widespread unrest and economic uncertainty, it's been quite the journey for all of us.

In response to the pandemic, I made a decision that felt right to my core: all 30-plus personal finance courses on the Clever Girl Finance platform would be made permanently free. So many people were struggling to get back on their feet or stay afloat, and it was clear that financial resources were more crucial than ever. This move was my way of giving back to the community that had supported Clever Girl Finance's growth and a way of providing support to women who needed these resources. It also allowed me to stay true to our mission at Clever Girl Finance – empowering women to achieve financial wellness. And with over 600,000 course enrollments and counting, it's evident that it was the right call to make. It's also a strong indicator that women want to thrive with money.

As we continue to pick up the pieces and adapt to ongoing life and global challenges, many are finding themselves reassessing their financial strategies in the wake of these turbulent times, so there's no better time than right now to bring you an updated and expanded version of *Clever Girl Finance: Ditch Debt, Save Money, and Build Real Wealth.*

I wrote the first version of this book to showcase that being successful with money doesn't have to be complicated or confusing and to empower women to achieve financial success so they can live life on their own terms. This updated and expanded edition remains true to that goal.

Throughout this book, you'll find fresh insights tailored to today's financial landscape and actionable tips that you can put into practice right away. While it's never been easier to save and invest than it is in today's world, it's also never been easier to fall into the comparison trap, overspend, or accumulate more debt, thanks to the ever-tempting world of social media, one-click purchases, and mobile payment apps.

So whether you're looking to fine-tune your financial mindset, master the art of budgeting, tackle your debt, dip your toes into investing, or explore side hustles to boost your income, I have updated and expanded this book to help you make the best financial decisions for yourself and create (or update) your financial game plan to adapt to today's world.

Many of the women who read the first edition shared with me how much they loved being able to read about the experiences and success stories of other women they could relate to. And so based on their feedback, I've also added several brand-new stories from more amazing women who are crushing their life goals and financial goals. These stories will not only inspire you but also remind you that your financial dreams are well within reach, no matter where you are on your journey.

Now is the perfect time to take charge of your finances, and with the updated advice, tips, and real-life stories in this book, you've got a trusty guide to help you tackle whatever comes your way. Again, thank you so much for being here and for picking up a copy of this book.

Let's get started and make your goals a reality!

You Are in the Right Place

So you've picked up this book because its cover and title have piqued your interest. Or perhaps someone recommended it to you.

Either way, you're probably reading this because you could be doing better with your money and you want some inspiration (and education) to help you get to that place where you are truly happy about your financial picture now and into the future.

Ultimately, you want to be able to live your life on your own terms without having to worry about money all the time. You shouldn't have to settle for things and situations you don't want because you lack the finances and options to make changes.

Right?

Well, I've written this book for women just like you – women who are working hard to make a living. Regardless of what your income is currently or what your financial situation looks like, in this book I'll show you, step by step, what you need to do to get to that happy place where you have peace of mind about your finances.

I'll be challenging you to ditch the status quo of debt and living paycheck to paycheck, and I'll be sharing a ton of inspiration to help you jumpstart your journey toward financial success.

In addition to learning what it takes to build real wealth, you'll read several incredible stories from women just like you who have accomplished major feats by adjusting their mindsets, paying off debt, and saving money. They'll show you that you too can be successful with your finances, as long as you are ready and willing to put the work in.

Wherever you are on your journey to building wealth, I am more than certain you can get to the stage you desire – and I'm going to show you how.

How to Use This Book

This book is your guide to financial success. I want you to gain the most benefit from it, so I've put together a few tips to help you along the way. While there are many ways to read this book and act on the information on these pages, here is what I recommend:

- Plan to read it all the way through so you don't miss any valuable information. You'll get a good sense of the whole picture of improving your finances.
- Pace yourself as you read it and take it one chapter at a time, doing the suggested action items as you go along. Highlight, take notes, and bookmark anything you want to revisit. Completing these action items as you go will allow you to start working on your finances right away and stay motivated to keep going.
- Once you are done reading the book and completing the action items, come back and review your notes, action items, and bookmarks.
- Keep this book as a reference to answer questions or get unstuck when needed.
- If you'd like some extra guidance, you can leverage the worksheets and templates in the corresponding sections in the Clever Girl Finance workbook, *My Wealth Plan*, to work through your action items.

The goal is to get as much as you possibly can from this book to help you win big with your finances!

For additional resources, visit clevergirlfinance.com to check out our completely free personal finance courses and participate in our amazing community.

Introduction

You have what it takes.

#CLEVERGIRLSKNOW

I started Clever Girl Finance as a platform to empower women to take charge of their personal finances. I wanted to create a comfortable space for women to learn and have conversations about money without being judged, shamed, or pressed to show off. And most importantly, I wanted to provide a space that would allow us to be ourselves regardless of our backgrounds or our current financial or life situations. Today, Clever Girl Finance is one of the largest personal finance platforms for women in the U.S., and I'm so proud of how far we've come in achieving this goal of providing a space for women to learn and speak freely about money.

Creating a comfortable and nonjudgmental space has been of utmost priority to me because as women, in a world filled with standards and expectations, we keep so much bottled up. Sometimes being honest with ourselves and letting it all out is necessary.

We are more likely to talk about things like dating, relationships, sex, shopping, parenting, and reality TV than we are to talk about paying off debt, saving money, or investing – the latter of which is super-important to our long-term financial well-being and overall quality of life.

Why do we shy away from the money conversation so much? Well, as a woman I know how hard it can be to talk about money because:

- We don't want to feel judged or shamed by the money mistakes we've made.
- We think other women are doing better with their money than we are because their lives look perfect in real life and on social media.
- Money is not a topic that we really grew up talking about, and so having those money conversations is not exactly second nature.
- We think talking about money is just way too personal.

These reasons plus several others are what get in the way of achieving our financial success.

Men, on the other hand, are the complete opposite. I mean, put five guys in a room and they'll talk about everything from sports to business to beer to women to money and they won't even give it a second thought. Why shouldn't we, as women, be that comfortable about having those same conversations about money? We are just as smart, we are just as successful, and we most certainly work just as darn hard for our dollars.

As the Clever Girl Finance Tribe has grown, I've received a lot of flak about how good money management, saving, investing, and building wealth is not just a "woman's thing." But in all honesty, I'm really not fazed by that criticism. I do believe it needs to be a "woman's thing."

Yes, building wealth applies to everyone – there's no dispute there – but I'm tired of our specific needs being ignored by the finance industry. I'm even more tired of seeing financial products and services designed by men from the male-dominated finance industry coated in pink and automatically termed "for women" because, well, that's not how it works for us.

I mean, I love pink, but it takes more than a pink coating for money topics to be relatable to us as women and for our financial needs to be met. And in so many instances, the products and services that exist today just don't cut it – especially in regard to the unique factors that affect us as women when it comes to our finances.

Those one-size-fits-all groupings that come with set standards? We don't quite fit into them – sorry.

Given all the unique (and sometimes negative) factors affecting us as women when it comes to our success with money, we need to make money "our thing" and deal with it "our way" in order for us to be able to build wealth. And more importantly, we need to be able to live life on our terms.

But what factors am I talking about?

Well, for one thing, we are earning more money on average than we have ever earned before. Many of us are heads of our households or, if we are in relationships, many of us earn significantly more than our partners or spouses.

However, despite us earning more than ever before, we are paid significantly less for doing the same work as our male counterparts in nearly every single occupation and industry and we continue to face an uphill battle when it comes to equal pay. On average, women earn about 18% less than men.[1] If we break it down by demographics, the numbers are even worse: Black women earn 36% less[2] and Hispanic women earn almost 48% less.[3] These numbers have not shifted much at all in the six years since I wrote the first edition of this book.

On top of that, we are living longer than men by an average of 5–10 years, which means we actually need more money for our financial well-being in retirement than men will. But stats show that, despite living longer, women have only 70% of the income that men have during retirement[4] as a result of the gender wage gap and, in turn, the subsequent investment gap; and so, because we don't earn as much, the women who do invest can't invest as much.[5]

And I haven't even gotten into the emotional side of things. As women, we tend to be more emotional beings – at least more so than men. That makes us big givers – not only are we more likely to give to charity and buy more extravagant gifts, but we're less likely to fight for a promotion or ask for more in a salary negotiation.

---

[1] https://www.pewresearch.org/short-reads/2023/03/01/gender-pay-gap-facts/

[2] https://www.cbcfinc.org/blog/closing-the-gap-reflecting-on-black-womens-equal-pay-day-and-the-path-forward/

[3] https://nwlc.org/resource/equal-pay-for-latinas

[4] https://www.aauw.org/issues/equity/retirement/

[5] https://www.femaleinvest.com/magazine/gender-investing-gap

But wait a minute, what about things like retail therapy? More women than men admit to shopping to make themselves feel better – and many admit to doing it because they want to make others feel happy. However, despite what might be perpetuated in the media and in popular marketing, just because we enjoy retail therapy doesn't mean the stereotype that all women are frivolous and excessive spenders is true. In fact, according to a researched article by the *New York Times*, frivolous or excessive spending has nothing to do with gender[6] and the Consumer Expenditure Surveys from the U.S. Bureau of Labor Statistics prove it.[7]

Keep in mind that when we do spend, women are typically paying more for the same exact products and services, from insurance to dry cleaning, clothing and feminine care purchases to major expenses like insurance. And while many states have banned this gender-based price discrimination, also known as the "pink tax," it continues to exist.[8]

I could go on and on with these factors, stating studies and statistics, but let's not get carried away. It's not a bad thing to be emotional, giving, or happy to spend. In fact, women are generally good with money. Like, really good with money. With the right tools, knowledge, and support, we are incredible savers and investors. The responses to our recurring Clever Girl Finance Women and Money Survey support the fact that women understand the importance of building wealth and are interested in investing, with 68% of respondents saying they actively invest for the future.[9] We also take more calculated risks and are more patient when it comes to reaping returns. Being emotionally aware isn't our downfall – it's our secret weapon.

---

[6] https://www.nytimes.com/2019/10/04/us/myth-frivolous-female-spender.html

[7] https://www.bls.gov/cex/tables.htm

[8] https://money.usnews.com/money/personal-finance/taxes/articles/the-pink-tax-costs-women-thousands-of-dollars-over-their-lifetimes

[9] https://www.clevergirlfinance.com/women-and-money/

The majority of us want to learn more about or do better with managing our money. We want to do better with saving and investing – so what is holding us back from our financial success?

More than likely, ourselves: our self-doubt, discomfort, fear, lack of knowledge, lack of support – the list goes on. But here's a secret:

If you really want to build wealth, regardless of whatever factors are at play, you totally can.

Yes, girl, you.

Regardless of where you are with your finances right now and despite all the factors I just listed, you can be debt free with solid savings and investments and live a fabulous life of your choosing while you're at it.

My goal with this book is to help you take charge of your finances, ditch debt, save money, and build real wealth so you can be in control of the life you really want to live. You can shop when you want to, feel free to buy gifts you want to give, and show all the people who think you can't succeed that you can. It might seem out of reach right at this moment, but you have what it takes to get there. You just took a major step by picking up this book.

Now that you're here, I'm going to teach you exactly how to improve your relationship with money, create a plan to pay off your debt, and save some serious money so you can start living your life on your own terms.

I will, however, be honest and tell you right from the start that I have no get-rich-quick schemes or magic tricks to share with you. In fact, becoming financially stable is certainly not going to be easy. But I can tell you, firsthand, that I've done it. And if I can, so can you. You are more than capable of getting your finances to a happy place.

My Story

The best way to predict the future is to create the one you want.

#CLEVERGIRLSKNOW

So what led me to this place of empowering women to achieve their own financial success? Well, let me take you way back. Growing up, I was the last of four children and the only girl. My father was the breadwinner, and my mother stayed at home.

She got married really young, at just 19, and soon started a family. I was born in Vienna, the gorgeous capital city of Austria, where my family relocated due to a life-changing job opportunity my father got after working for several years as a college professor and then as a civil servant in Nigeria.

As a result of my family's relocation and my father's better pay, we got to go to good schools, my parents had nice cars, we lived in a nice house, and our family was taken care of. I wouldn't describe my family as rich, but my father was able to afford many of the nicer things for us. His biggest priority was to give his children the best education possible.

As time went by, my mother began to notice certain things about herself and within her community of friends. For instance, she realized she didn't have much insight into our family finances because my father managed all the money. The same applied to her friends – they didn't know much about the details of their family finances, either.

My mother didn't quite like the fact that she had to ask my father for money to do everything. It wasn't that my father didn't give her the money; rather, it was that he made all the major financial decisions. She wanted to be able to make her own contributions toward our household and put money aside for herself.

Since she only had a high school diploma when she got married, my mother decided to go to college and get a degree, so she could eventually get a job that allowed her to make a significant contribution to our family's finances. As the years went by, she went on to get an undergraduate degree, a master's degree, and several professional certifications, which set the stage for her to take control of her earning potential and her financial future.

Over this same period, while my mother was setting the stage for her own financial security, she observed the financial problems her friends were having. The friends whose marriages ended in divorce wound up with no financial support. I watched my mother console many friends who were trying to figure out exactly how to start over with little or no money. Similar things would happen if one of their husbands passed away. They had no clue as to what assets existed or where any of the money was. In some cases, their husband's family would come in and take over, ousting them from the situation, again with zero financial support.

Thankfully, my parents stayed married (and celebrated their fiftieth anniversary not long ago). But with these experiences, my mother had made up her mind that she never wanted to be in any of those situations. So she became the hustle queen.

After my father's job tenure was over, my family relocated back to Nigeria and my mother, who had now completed her college education, began to get her hustle on. She worked as an investment banker, owned a hair salon, set up a typing school (anyone remember the typewriter?), was the principal of a girls' school, had a Coca-Cola franchise, considered starting a bakery, and ventured into so many other small businesses over the subsequent years that I can't even remember them all. Her main goal was financial peace of mind – and she was serious about it. While all this was going on, my father was spending the money he was earning paying for my older brothers' high school and college educations at the best schools he could afford.

Then something unexpected changed our financial stability. Just before I graduated high school and started thinking about which colleges I would apply to in the United States, my father was forced to retire 15 years earlier than he'd planned. Since he'd spent so much of his income on my brothers' education, he hadn't put much away for his own retirement. Thankfully, we would still be okay financially – my father was entitled to a pension and had a few assets and investments to keep the family afloat. However, our lifestyle would have to be downgraded in a major way.

This meant moving from our nice house to a tiny apartment. It meant that instead of multiple cars we would have just one car. And most devastating of all for me, it meant I would not be going to college abroad like I had dreamed.

Economic instability in Nigeria at the time meant there was no telling when I'd graduate if I went to college there. This is where my mother, the hustle queen, stepped in and changed my perspective about money forever.

She decided that I would be able to go to college abroad and that she would be paying for it with her own money that she had worked hard for and saved up all those years at the expense of delaying her retirement. She paid for all four years of my international college tuition, while continuing to work throughout, and gave me the opportunity to go to college in Austria (where I started), England, and then the United States (where I graduated).

The agreement I had with her was that my grades were not to be compromised – in other words, I dared not mess up – and I would get a job and apply for scholarships where possible. I was also reminded that this was an opportunity and a privilege, not a right – something I never forgot! This gift from my mother is one I am forever grateful for and will never take for granted.

I was able to get a partial scholarship for a year while in college in Austria, which helped ease the tuition costs my mother had to pay during that time. And I graduated college with flying colors – I made my mother proud!

I acknowledge that I am extremely lucky to have a parent pay for my college education, and I know many of you reading this are tackling student loan debt – a serious topic that I cover in detail in this book with the help of a student loan expert, who, by the way, also shares her incredible money story.

The privilege I was afforded, however, is not the point of this story. Seeing my mother make this sacrifice for me changed my life.

It laid a foundation for me to become financially successful, independent of anyone else. Her actions helped me realize that having my own money would open the doors for me to be able to make my own decisions and live my life on my own terms.

I saw that having money would give me options, and I would never find myself stuck in an unfavorable position (like my mother's friends were) if I planned carefully. She gave me valuable lessons that I can now pass on to my own children. However, it has taken a lot of trial and error to get me to this point where I can tell you my story.

Despite the great money lessons I learned from my mother, I still managed to make a few of my own money mistakes when I left home for college. Because I'd never really been thrown out in the world on my own to make any serious money decisions, I had a lot to learn.

Upon arrival in the United States for my final year of college, I had no clue about credit cards. They weren't something my parents used (at the time, credit cards were not a thing in Nigeria), nor had they ever been presented to me as a college student in Austria. However, at my very first college job fair in the United States, I couldn't ignore the credit card table – I mean, they were giving out free T-shirts! I happily applied for my first credit card despite my mother's warnings and without fully understanding what I was getting into. I quickly maxed out that credit card and ended up paying a ridiculous rate of 24.99% on my $2,000 balance, which took me forever to pay back with a part-time campus job earning $8 an hour and working around 15 hours a week. The Credit Card Accountability Responsibility and Disclosure Act (CARD Act) has since been put in place to protect minors and students from these types of solicitations.[1]

[1] https://www.ftc.gov/legal-library/browse/statutes/credit-card-accountability-responsibility-disclosure-act-2009-credit-card-act

While my line of credit on that card was not large, upon realization of how much interest I would be paying, combined with the fact that I only earned around $120 a week and still needed to buy groceries and pay for my personal needs, I had many sleepless nights! It felt like I owed a million dollars and would never be able to pay it off.

And let's not even talk about my very ridiculous and very expensive designer handbag collection I began to acquire a few years after graduating from college when I started earning my first real salary. Not only was it very expensive, but I hardly ever actually used the handbags! I held on to them for years before eventually selling them off.

I've also had to work through my own personal money roadblocks I've carried with me from childhood. If you're struggling financially, you probably read all about my childhood above and thought I was incredibly fortunate. And I was. But one drawback of the way I was raised is that I had a lot given to me that I didn't have to work for. As a young adult, I felt entitled to those same things, but I didn't understand what the true cost of that entitlement would be.

I didn't know how to spend smartly or how to use credit to my advantage. I made mistake after mistake and had to learn how to manage money on my own. However, despite those mistakes, I never lost my focus on building long-term wealth.

For example, I was able to save over $100,000 in a little over three years right after I graduated from college. This was a huge deal because I made nothing close to six figures, and I never imagined I would be able to save that much. (I'll share more later on about exactly how I did this.)

I learned about investing in the stock market and in real estate, two topics I initially thought I would never understand. Now I'm focused on building generational wealth for my children. And you can get there, too!

As I've gotten older, I've also gotten wiser. The decisions I make about money are more thoughtful. I like nice things, but not at the expense of my future or my children's future; these are nonnegotiable for me. I've also started to see some of the same things that were happening with my mother's friends repeat themselves with women around me.

The biggest recurring theme I see when it comes to women and money is that we are not getting as involved as we should when it comes to our financial well-being.

And I get it. Money can be intimidating, overly complicated, stressful, and sometimes a huge chore – but it doesn't have to be. I'll show you how to make it easy. I went from having a fortunate childhood to being an indebted student and now, finally, to a financially secure mom and entrepreneur. On my personal journey, I've learned so much about paying off debt, saving money, and planning for my financial future. And in this book, I'm sharing with you what I've learned. But that's just my story.

In this book, you'll get to read the stories of other women, all of whom come from very different backgrounds yet have one thing in common – regardless of their backgrounds and their history with money, they have all achieved financial success.

Your experience with money and your financial role models growing up may differ from mine. Maybe you grew up with more privilege than I did. Maybe your family has always struggled. Either way, your story, both the positives and negatives of it, tie into your current relationship with money today. In order to get to the point where you are in a happy space with your finances, you need to take a look back at your financial history and address your money roadblocks head on.

So, what's your story? Let me ask you a few questions to get those thoughts rolling in your mind:

- How did your parents deal with their money?
- Did they openly discuss money matters or financial challenges?
- What were the positives or negatives about money in your life when you were growing up?

- What's the strongest money memory or emotional experience tied to money you have from growing up that's stuck with you to this day?
- How do you think it affects the way you deal with money today?
- Did your parents instill any specific financial rules or values?
- What about money makes you anxious or stressed?
- What are the key money roadblocks you face?

Understanding your story will help you see where you struggle and what causes your anxiety and worry about money. You want to make sure that as you start working on your plan with this book to get on the path to building real wealth, you address any roadblocks from your history with money, so you can get comfortable about where you are headed with your finances.

Take Action

1. Take some time to write down your responses to the questions I've asked about your history as it relates to money, and your current financial attitudes and behaviors. Be as detailed and honest as possible in your answers.
2. Read over your answers and reflect on your thoughts and feelings about what you've written.
3. Once you've done a thorough reflection, write down one to three key actions you can take to overcome your roadblocks and assign time frames over the next few days and months to take action.

PART I

The Start

Clever girls know . . . It starts with you and where you are right now.

#CLEVERGIRLSKNOW

Your *What* and Your *Why*

Decide that you can and then you will.

Have you ever tried to lose a few pounds? You probably decided on a workout plan and started out on a high note, only to find yourself, a few days or weeks later, indulging in a fully loaded carb and sugar party. And those workouts – well, they became fewer and farther between, maybe even nonexistent. Sound familiar?

I'm sure we've all been there at one time or the other – at least I have. Go on, it's okay to admit it.

I've been the girl who's said, "I'm going to lose 10 pounds no matter what!" I got the gym membership, signed up for the classes . . . I even went out and got my retail therapy on by getting brand-new super-cute neon-colored workout gear. I was totally convinced that the mere (blinding) sight of the neon in my closet would be the motivator I needed to get me to the gym every day.

Yeah, right.

When it really came down to it and the euphoria from buying that hot neon mess (which I'd never be caught dead wearing at the gym) wore off, I was back to my carb and sugar party, singing, "Woe is me, I'm just not meant to fit into those size 27 jeans."

The real problem? I just wasn't ready. I didn't want it bad enough.

Losing weight is not always easy. It takes a certain level of determination, working out (ugh), eating healthy, and a strong resolve to keep going, even on the suckiest of days when a tub of ice cream is the only thing that can make you feel better.

However, when you do stick to your plan and see the numbers on the scale going down, you're fitting into jeans that you could barely zip up a couple months ago, and people are complimenting you about how fabulous you look, you feel great! You realize that putting in all that effort was worth it, and you are happier for it.

Well, when it comes to your finances and building wealth, things work in a similar way.

Just like with getting in shape, getting your finances in order does not happen overnight (if it did, we'd all be rich by morning!) and it's certainly not always fun. Sometimes it can be downright annoying, frustrating, and stressful – but getting things in order is 100% worth it. What's more, it's very possible for you to do. The thing is, you first have to decide that you are ready. You have to want to get to a better place with your money badly enough.

So where do you begin?

You begin with the thoughts you think and the decisions you make around what you want to accomplish. In this case, it's wanting to get to a place where you achieve financial success and have peace of mind about your finances. Yes, as you work on building wealth it's super-important to focus on having a plan for emergencies, learning to budget, paying off debt, setting savings goals, and investing – but before you start making those plans, it's important to have the right mindset and focus in place.

In other words, first and foremost, you have to decide that you can.

That debt you have that seems so incredibly large – you can pay it off.

Those savings goals that seem so out of reach – you can reach and even surpass them.

Once you've decided that you can, the next step is to get clear on your *why*.

If you aren't quite sure, your *why* is essentially the driving force that keeps you going, especially when life starts *life-ing* and everything in you wants to quit. It provides you with a sense of direction and is tied to your purpose, which in turn ties into you living a fulfilled life. It can also help you overcome your fears and doubts because you'll be reminded of your purpose, which is bigger than any fear or doubt you might have.

Finding your *why* is about being honest with yourself and getting clear on what truly makes you happy and the deeper motivation that causes you to want certain things in your life. It should be the reason for the goals you choose to pursue.

Keep in mind that you can have multiple *whys*. You can even have a *why* associated with different aspects of your life, like your family and relationships, your career, your health and wellness, your personal growth, and, of course, your finances.

For example, when it comes to the goals you have that are tied to your family and relationships, your *why* might be to create beautiful and long-lasting memories, spend quality time together, and cultivate deeper connections and emotional intimacy.

Your *why* in your career might be to make a positive impact through the work that you do, find fulfilment through work, and be a strong leader in your field who inspires others.

For your health and wellness, your *why* might be to improve your mental and emotional well-being, improve your physical fitness, and reduce stress and overwhelm in your life.

For your personal growth it might be to continue to develop and improve on specific skills, build up your self-confidence and communication skills, and cultivate mindfulness and a deeper sense of self.

Now when it comes to your finances, it's important that you really spend the time to lay out your *why*. This is because your finances pretty much touch every aspect of your life in one way or another. While not the sole factor, money is a key contributor to:

- The quality of life you live with your family and the experiences you have
- Your ability to acquire the education and skills needed for a career path
- Improving your health and wellness through access to good nutrition, good healthcare, a good living environment and more

And so, with that said, your *why* (or *whys*) when it comes to money might include:

- Creating financial security and stability for you and your family so you don't have to worry about money
- Becoming debt free
- Starting your own business to expand your earning potential
- Being able to fund travel to create new experiences
- Retiring early to enjoy more of life while you are still young and healthy
- Building generational wealth for your children and their children
- Giving back financially to positively impact the life of others in your family, community, or through charitable endeavors

TIP

Having a clear "why" provides you with motivation and direction, so make sure your "why" is personal and truly meaningful to you.

Now that you know what a *why* is and why having one is so important, ask yourself, "Why do I want to succeed with my finances?" This will involve you doing some serious reflection and might take some time, but it's an important step you don't want to skip.

Your *why* is personal to you. It's not about what other people expect you to want, what society's standards are, or who your Instagram feed says you should be. It's about what truly matters to you and what brings you fulfillment.

It's important to keep in mind that your *why* may also change or evolve over time as you navigate different life stages and experiences. This is normal and if it happens to you, it's okay.

Personally, my *why* has changed several times from when I was single and it was all about me, to when I got married and I added on new joint *whys* with my husband, to when I became a mother and adjusted some of my *whys* based on the legacy we want to create for our children.

As human beings, we are constantly growing and evolving, so if you feel a shift in what drives you and gives you fulfilment, adjust your *why* accordingly.

Your *why* will also tie into establishing your core values, which we'll delve into in more detail in Chapter 2.

As you go on this journey to financial wellness, it's inevitable that you will face challenges and setbacks. However, regardless of what challenges or setbacks you may face, making up your mind that "you can" and establishing your "why" is the foundation of what will keep you motivated to put in the effort.

You'll have to come up with ideas to make things work. You'll have to do things that might not necessarily be ideal. You may make mistakes along the way. But as long as you lean on your ability, are aware of your *why*, and are not afraid to fail, and as long as you understand that within every failure is a lesson that can propel you forward, you can do whatever you put your mind to.

But first you have to want your financial success, however you choose to define it, badly enough.

Take Action

1. Write down the answers to the questions below:
   - What it is you want to accomplish with your finances and other aspects of your life?
   - Why do you want to accomplish it? What is your *why*? (Remember, you can have multiple *whys*.)
   - What are the things holding you back? What fears might you have?
2. Now pause and consciously decide that you can do this regardless of any setbacks or fears you have.

3. Next, write down one simple action you can take right now or in the next few days to counter each one of those fears.
4. Finally, get a copy of your *why* (or *whys*) and put it somewhere you'll see it every day as a constant reminder of why you need to succeed. Be sure to carve out time to reflect on your *why* periodically.

CHAPTER 1
Your Mindset

Forget the mistakes, remember the lessons.

#CLEVERGIRLSKNOW

LET GO OF YOUR MONEY MISTAKES

I have personally made a ton of money mistakes. From overspending my budget to buying things I don't need to making poor investment choices, I've been there and done that.

You've probably made a few yourself. But now you are here and you've made the decision that you can be financially successful. It doesn't stop there. You are going to have to continuously work on developing your mindset to keep it in top shape, just like you would any other muscle in your body.

Money mistakes are all too common. Yes, we've all wasted money. Yes, we've all made decisions that have had a long-term impact on our finances.

All that overspending on unplanned travel, nights out, clothes we don't need. . .

Loaning money to that family member or friend and never getting it back. . .

Cosigning that loan. . .

Not saving or investing as a priority. . .

Any of these mistakes sound familiar?

The trouble with our money mistakes is that too many of us allow them to keep us stuck. We allow them to prevent us from making positive progress with our finances. We get so caught up with being afraid to make new mistakes or we end up judging ourselves for those past mistakes so much that it becomes too hard to take that next step.

We feel ashamed and embarrassed about our money slipups. We beat ourselves up, wondering how we could have been so careless. And to make matters worse, we let others chime in with their judgments as well. It's like a never-ending cycle of self-criticism that can show up in our lives in different ways.

Maybe you find yourself constantly splurging, trying to lift your spirits in the moment. Or perhaps you avoid dealing with your finances altogether, convinced things will never improve. And then there's the sneaky habit of hiding your spending from loved ones because you know you're going overboard. It's tough, but these behaviors can creep in when we're feeling the weight of our money mistakes.

The thing is, wherever you are today with your finances is pretty much what it is. The big question is, what are you going to do next? What are you going to do about where you are right now? Are you going to keep dwelling on the past and all the things you did wrong? Or are you going to look to the future and figure out exactly how to make this right using your experience as a steppingstone?

If there's anything I've learned from my mother, it's that regardless of what mistakes you make and no matter how foolish they are, life goes on – and the direction you go after the realization is entirely up to you. And this means taking a good hard look at those mistakes, doing an assessment, and gleaning the lessons.

For me, the biggest money mistake I've made was the very large and very expensive designer handbag collection I once owned.

After aggressively saving for a few years, I had accumulated over $100,000 in savings. I was earning well over six figures and I felt like I deserved something nice – a Chanel handbag. After all, I wasn't a big shopper and I didn't really spend my money on anything expensive, so why not?

I vividly remember my first purchase. It was a Chanel classic flap with black caviar leather and gold hardware. It cost $2850. I was ecstatic about it and proud of my purchase. I wore it often and kept it in pristine condition. It was my prized possession.

But for some reason, it wasn't enough for me to have just one Chanel handbag. I mean, just one? Who does that? (Insert sarcastic look here.) So a few months later, I just had to have another one. And then another few months went by and I "needed" another one. This cycle continued for a few years.

Every few months, I reduced the amount I was putting into my savings to purchase another Chanel handbag in another fabulous color for thousands of dollars. But unlike that first Chanel handbag that I used all the time, the more bags I bought, the less I used them, until I was barely using anything in my now large collection. Not only was my cost per wear out of control, but I had thousands of dollars' worth of leather handbags sitting in my closet for no reason.

I battled with the guilt of excessiveness. I felt silly, but I would go back and forth in my mind about why I deserved them, why I needed to keep them, and how I had a good amount of savings anyway.

But then it dawned on me: Whom was I fooling with a closet full of handbags that I wasn't using? I wasn't a real housewife of anywhere, nor was I a fashion icon of any sort or a celebrity required to make frequent public appearances. What did I really need all these handbags for?

Shortly after, and with great difficulty (even though now I wonder what was so difficult about it), I made the decision that every single one of those Chanel handbags had to go.

Luckily for me, I was able to sell every single one for close to what I paid for them (and even double for some). Including that very first black Chanel bag I bought, which I sold for $5700 thanks to Chanel's crazy price increases.

Sounds like a winning situation, right? I sold the bags and made a profit. I can call it a win if I want to make myself feel better. The truth of it, though, is that it was a major loss.

Let me explain.

Around the same time I was buying handbags, I had started learning about investing (oh, the contradiction!), and one of the stocks I was interested in was Amazon. I barely invested anything in it because I was too busy buying handbags.

Well, guess what? If I'd taken the money I spent on just that first Chanel handbag and put it toward buying more Amazon stock, that $2850 alone would have increased to well over $35,000 at the time that I wrote the first edition of this book. Fast forward to today, as I write this updated and expanded version of this book, the price of that same Chanel handbag is now $12,750 before sales tax. (Yes, you read that right, Chanel price increases have been steadily insane!). But if I'd bought the Amazon stock and left it alone, I would have about $100,000 now. And I seriously doubt that I would have been able to sell what would now be an "old" Chanel handbag, even in excellent condition, for today's current price of $12,750.

And let's not even talk about how much I would have right now if I hadn't bought any of those handbags to begin with and invested all that money in Amazon stock instead. Yeah, that one stings.

Again, when it comes to money mistakes, this takes the cake for me – but I can't cry over spilled milk forever. Instead of staying there and wallowing about my losses, I decided to let go, refocus, and get back on top of my money goals. Yes, I still love handbags and I still splurge now and again, but never at the expense of my financial goals and definitely not in the excessive manner in which I used to.

Maybe your mistakes are minor – or maybe they're even worse than mine. Either way, you can come back from it. The whole point of letting go of your money mistakes is to actually let go. Wipe the slate clean, reset, refocus, throw the self-judgment out the window, and move forward.

Remember, mistakes are inevitable and are part of our growth process as human beings. So change your lens on how you view mistakes and instead look at them as opportunities for growth and learning, rather than failures.

Here are three steps you can take right now to help you let go of your money mistakes so you can start making real progress toward your goals.

1. Acknowledge your mistakes and forgive yourself.

   In order to get ahead, you are going to have to forgive yourself for your money mistakes, take the lessons you've learned, and keep it moving.

   Yes, mistakes happen. Everyone has made bad decisions around their money – even the world's wealthiest people. I can guarantee that any well-known wealthy person you can think of has made at least one major mistake with their money at some point on their financial journey. Mistakes are part of the learning process in life and they provide you with an opportunity to grow.

So acknowledge where you went wrong, take ownership, figure out what to do to make things right (on your own or with the right support), and end the self-judgment. It's time to move forward and let go of any resentment or guilt you are feeling. The pity party is over.

Even if you wind up making the same or similar mistakes again, give yourself grace. Your approach should be to rinse and repeat the process of acknowledging the mistake, learning how to improve, and implementing the lessons until you get past your error.

2. Decide that it's time to take action toward change.

   Next, you have to be willing to change and be committed to seizing the moment to start working on revamping your finances, right now. No more waiting for perfect – the perfect job, the perfect city, the perfect relationship. Just start.

   This means creating a plan to address any consequences or setbacks because of your past mistakes and setting clear and achievable goals (we'll talk more about this in the next chapter).

   This also means if you can only save $5 a week right now, save that $5. It means if you can only put $10 toward your debt this week, make that $10 payment until you get to the point where you are able to ramp it up. It's less about the amount and more about the consistent action.

3. Get motivated.

   When you start working on your financial goals, there will be a period of euphoria. You'll get that fresh sense of excitement that comes with new goals. However, as you go through the motions of accomplishing your goals and as time goes by, you are going to need continuous motivation to help you stay focused. That's what will keep you going when it comes to the things you want to achieve in your life, and you have to be mindful of where you seek it.

Some ways to stay motivated include finding an accountability partner, reading books, listening to podcasts, or watching videos that keep you excited as you make progress on your financial goals.

Take Action

1. Make a list of every money mistake you've made that you can think of.
2. Next, write out the lessons you can take away from each of those mistakes.
3. Take a deep breath, forgive yourself, and let it go. Scream it out loud if necessary – it works wonders, I promise!
4. Make a list of ways you can stay motivated, books you can read, podcasts you can listen to, video series you can watch, and people you can connect with.
5. Set a timeframe to start working through that list.

BECOMING EMOTIONALLY BALANCED FOR A POSITIVE MONEY MINDSET

When it comes to improving your personal finances, your money mindset is a critical and foundational piece and your emotions tie directly into it.

Your goals may revolve around becoming debt-free, saving money, investing, or getting to seven figures in assets, but without emotional balance, it will be difficult for you to accomplish any of these goals, especially since it is almost impossible for you to avoid the wide range of emotions that you will feel.

But what does emotional balance really mean? It is essentially your ability to balance or regulate your emotions, both pleasant and unpleasant, to maintain a state of positive mental well-being.[1] And having a positive mindset is part of that positive mental well-being.

These days all it takes is a quick Google search (or AI query) and within seconds you'll be provided with a wide variety of results, giving you step-by-step guidance on everything you need to do to get you closer to your money goals. But if you've ever attempted to accomplish a difficult goal and failed, you know that it requires a lot more than a step-by-step guide telling you what to do to successfully meet that goal, right?

A ton of emotions are involved on your financial journey and if I'm being honest, it can be hard to keep all those emotions in check while you take on the sometimes difficult and long-term task of improving your finances and building wealth.

Money has a huge impact on how we get to live our lives. And it's only natural that we tend to attach a great deal of emotion to it. But sometimes these emotions can be negative, which can lead to bigger problems, such as emotional spending or getting into debt. In fact, a recent study by Northwestern Mutual found that, on average, 36% of Americans feel anxiety about their finances, with the percentages being much higher for Gen Z (44%) and Millennials (53%).[2] And as you are probably already aware, money is a dominant source of stress, right up there with personal relationships and having a job.

Not being able to keep your emotions in check can lead to feelings of unworthiness, low self-esteem, imposter syndrome, and feeling like a failure even when you are actually making progress.

I've personally struggled in the past with maintaining my emotions when it came to my finances. My unchecked emotions had me feeling like I could not achieve my financial goals, allowed me to entertain a scarcity mindset for periods of time when things weren't going according to plan, and even let other

---

[1] https://www.nhsfife.org/services/all-services/child-and-adolescent-mental-health-service-camhs/things-to-try/emotional-balance

[2] More than a third (36%) of Americans say uncertainty about their finances keeps them up at night at least monthly.

people's negativity influence my motivation. However, in addition to gaining clarity on my *why,* digging deep into my money blocks, and learning from and letting go of my mistakes, I've been able to maintain a positive money mindset by learning how to be emotionally balanced, especially when it comes to anxiety, fear, anger, regret, and even jealousy (yup, I get jealous sometimes too)!

So, let's talk about these emotions and how to achieve and maintain your own emotional balance.

Anxiety and Fear

Anxiety and fear are at the top of the list of negative emotions, and having financial anxiety or a fear of money is all too common. Remember, more than a third of Americans feel anxious about their money regularly.

Maybe you worry about how you'll earn enough money and how you'll pay your bills. Or perhaps you worry that you'll lose what you have or that you can't manage your money well enough. You may be worrying so much about your financial situation that it becomes very stressful, and as a result you avoid your finances altogether.

But you can balance your emotions of anxiety and fear by being intentional and getting out of your own way. When you start feeling anxious or fearful about your money, instead of staying stuck, ask yourself, what can I do to get past this? If you worry about not being able to pay your bills, work with what you can control and create a plan. This may mean calling your utility company or loan servicer to ask for a grace period or a payment plan. Worried about forgetting to pay your bills? Automate your bill payments so those bills can get paid on time. Wondering where all your money is going every month? Start tracking your spending on a daily basis.

If it's all just too overwhelming, talk to someone you trust, or consult with a financial advisor or even a therapist (no shame – I love my therapist) to help you get past the overwhelm. Just don't allow yourself to stay stuck in anxiety or fear.

Regret and Anger

You know those shoulda, woulda, coulda feelings? Well, those are the feelings that lead to regret and anger about your finances. You may have regrets about going on multiple shopping sprees and not saving enough money. Or perhaps you have regrets about opening up those credit card accounts and racking up all that debt.

You hold on to these regrets and then the anger sets in. You ask yourself, "What was I thinking?!" You get mad at yourself for being irresponsible with your money, for letting yourself get into so much debt, and for not catching yourself sooner.

But one thing that's necessary to remember is that you can learn from your financial mistakes and do better. Instead of regret, focus on forgiveness. Forgive yourself for your past financial mistakes, take the lessons (you'll learn several), and keep it moving. Ever heard the saying "There's no use crying over spilled milk?" Well, there's no point in regret because it doesn't get you anywhere.

It's okay to get mad, but channel those angry feelings into good use. Get so mad that your mindset around your debt becomes one of "never again." Get so mad that you create a solid budget and strategy that ensures you never fall back into your old ways of poorly managing your finances.

Shame and Embarrassment

Next up are shame and embarrassment. Maybe you feel shame because you think people will judge you for your money mistakes. Or you feel embarrassed about your current financial situation and judge yourself for it.

We want to look good in front of our friends and family. We don't want to admit our money situation isn't that great, especially when society (and social media) are telling us what we should have accomplished financially by a certain age.

Well, as I mentioned earlier, everyone has made money mistakes, even the smartest and wealthiest people in the world, and believe me when I say they've made several. Just do a Google search on your favorite successful people. Anyone who tells you they've never made a mistake with their money is either lying or just hasn't made one yet and believe me, they will.

The key to balancing emotions from shame is to realize that you have nothing to prove to anyone but yourself. It's time to let go of the shame and self-judgment and instead find your inner strength to take the lessons you've learned and move forward.

Jealousy

Jealousy also comes in a milder form known as "keeping up with the Joneses." The grass always looks greener on the other side, until you get to the other side and realize things aren't what they seem.

The trouble is, when people try to keep up, they end up living beyond their means, getting into debt, and pushing themselves much further away from their financial goals.

To balance your emotions around jealousy, focus on practicing gratitude and contentment, instead of focusing on what other people have that you don't. Take time each day to remind yourself of the things you wanted in the past that you now have. You can even start a gratitude journal or list that you add to every day.

When you start to feel jealous, channel those emotions into motivation to work harder, and do better within your means. And always remember, there are things you have that someone else is praying for.

If you relate to any of these emotions, know that it's human nature for us to feel the full gamut of emotions, both positive and negative. What matters more is that you can recognize when you start feeling these negative emotions so you can take intentional action to put a positive spin on them.

▶ TIP

When you start feeling negative emotions, acknowledge your feelings without self-judgment and instead focus on finding healthy ways to process and cope with them. For example, you can practice mindfulness by meditating, praying, journaling, or simply just focusing on the here and now.

MEET DR. CHAVONNE PEROTTE

Dr. Chavonne Perotte (http://drchavonne.com) is a life and marriage coach and a trained social science researcher with a doctorate from the Johns Hopkins Bloomberg School of Public Health. She is also the founder of RelateAble, LLC, a coaching practice that provides private coaching to women and couples all over the world.

Chavonne shares how having a negative mindset and lack mentality can impact finances, marriages, friendships, and more, including her own personal experience. She also shares how to overcome a lack mentality and embrace abundance without guilt.

How would you define a lack mentality?

I see it as not having enough and becoming preoccupied and hyper-focused with that as your current state. It's an endless cycle and spiral that puts people in an anxious state of feeling like they can never get ahead and that where they are now is not enough.

When you have a lack mentality because you live in this anxious state, it clouds your judgment, and it clouds your ability to come up with appropriate, effective, or creative solutions for anything, including improving your finances.

What has your personal experience been with having a lack mentality and how did you overcome it?

In my twenties, before I got married, I was one of those women who never looked at my finances at all. I just got the bills, and I prayed there would be enough money for what I needed to pay for. I would overdraw my account all the time because I wasn't aware of how much I had at any given moment.

When I got married, my husband and I kept our finances separate initially. We were both pretty established in our careers and so it worked well. But then we decided to have a family, so I stopped working temporarily before starting my own business. My husband is incredibly financially responsible and forward thinking. He had a lot of savings and operates mostly on cash. And so, when we began having conversations about money, it surfaced for me how "far behind" I was, and I felt a lot of shame about my previous money decisions. I had credit card debt, no savings, and I felt very inadequate about understanding and managing money.

What really helped with getting out of that lack mentality and being wise about how I use my money was asking myself, "What are the things I value?" "Is how I'm using my money in alignment with what I care about and what's important to me?" and "Is using my money in these ways going to help me achieve my long-term goals?" This shift took me out of feeling like I didn't have enough and reminded me that I did have enough when I focused on the things that were important to me.

You work with a lot of women and couples in your coaching practice. How have you seen lack mentality impact their finances and relationships?

I think the biggest barrier is the judgment couples can have toward each other in this area. We are inherently biased in our own perspective and ways of doing things. So when we partner with someone who has a different money mindset, it's easy to think, "They are wrong, and I am right." This can lead to control issues, and lack of equity in decision-making.

But what's really necessary is understanding the underlying factors that contribute to how anyone thinks about and handles money. When you can be more curious and seek to understand *why* your partner operates the way they do, and come together to find a mutual goal, money doesn't have to be an issue – no matter how much you have or are working to create.

How does one go from having a lack mentality to embracing abundance without guilt, especially when it comes to money?

It starts with recognizing that money is something that is necessary, and it's a tool to help you live the kind of life you want (and deserve to live). When you give your money a purpose you feel good about, and that truly represents the best of who you are as a person, there is nothing to feel guilty about. In fact, you will strive to create even more.

Making this shift also requires you to spend time truly being grateful and feeling sufficient right where you are with what you have today. Think about all the ways money is serving you, working for you, and supporting your life right now.

How does one involve a partner in embracing abundance?

The best way to influence a partner who might be in a different space with money than you are is by being the best example you can be of the benefits of an abundant mindset. We think shaming, controlling, and criticizing someone works, but it never does. Instead, the more space you give them to come to their own conclusions, to find the benefit in changing for themselves, the easier that growth process becomes for both of you.

Focus on what you can control. Share your wins in a genuine way without trying to convince them that they need to think the way you do. Offer a lot of grace and understanding while also taking empowered action on your own.

Dream bigger than big!

#CLEVERGIRLSKNOW

DREAM BIG: AFFIRM YOURSELF TO BEING WEALTHY

Now let's talk about the ideal life you want to live. If you want to turn your dreams into reality, you are going to have to lay them all out and start affirming yourself to being wealthy as you put in the work to accomplish your goals.

Personally, I'm a huge fan of affirmations. They help me get my head in the game and they serve as reminders of my *why*. I use affirmations in my day-to-day life around my financial goals, my business goals, my fitness goals, and other life goals I want to accomplish. They provide emotional support and encouragement as I make progress, and they are essentially another form of motivation for me.

The amazing thing about affirmations is that everything I have ever consistently affirmed that was tied to a "why" has happened in my life. From wanting to save large amounts of money, to building a successful business, to the home I live in with my family, it has happened and become a reality for me once I started affirming that it would.

But what exactly is an affirmation? Well, to put it simply, it's declaring something to be true. When you declare or affirm something, you are in conscious control of your thoughts because you get to really focus on what you are saying. Whenever you say an affirmation, you think it and see it in your mind. Creating short, powerful affirmations for your finances will turn your "I can't" into "I can," and help you get past your fears and translate your dreams into your reality.

So if I were to ask you what your dreams are and where you imagine your life a few years from now, what would your response be? Off the top of your head, you'd probably be able to give me a general idea of where you see yourself and what you'd like to have accomplished.

Perhaps you want to have a nice house on the beach or with a nice view of the city. Maybe you want to take luxury vacations with your family every year. Or maybe you want to help others by giving back financially or having the career or business of your dreams. Your list probably goes on.

But there's a problem with everything I've listed above – and it isn't particularly obvious. Those dreams are just a little bit too broad and general. And that rings true with the way most of us dream.

Yes, it's important to dream – and to dream big at that – but there's a difference between having your dreams become your reality and having your dreams stay out of reach: being specific with what you want out of life. You need to be razor sharp and crystal clear with your goals and affirmations if they are to become your reality.

Adding that level of clarity will help you determine what you truly want out of your life. You can filter out all the options and narrow in on the exact thing you want. You are much more likely to achieve what you set out to do because you have a clear focus on what to pursue – and what not to.

Becoming very clear on your goals and your dreams will help you achieve them, but there's a downside. You see, as you start to get more specific about your dreams, your limiting beliefs will set in. Thoughts like "I will never be able to achieve this," or "Why am I wasting my time? This will never happen," or "Girl, who? You? Please," will start to run through your mind on repeat. You'll need to train your mind to get rid of those thoughts whenever they come up and replace them with empowering ones. This is where affirmations come in. Positive affirmations build the mental muscles that can be incredibly powerful for achieving goals and making your dreams a reality.

As you create affirmations to support bringing your dreams to reality, it's important to keep the following in mind:

- Your affirmations should be short and concise.
- Your affirmations should be about your life and should be personal.

- They should be in the present tense.
- They should be positive.
- You should not compare yourself to anyone else when you create your affirmations.

Some examples of affirmations are:

- Money is attracted to my bank account every single day.
- I am credit card debt free.
- I make good money decisions and invest wisely.

Once you create these affirmations, you want to refer to them often, so keep them visible and accessible. Save them as your phone screen saver, tape them to your bathroom mirror, put them on your fridge. The more you affirm, the more you believe you can, so the more you will!

TIP

A great way to remember to say your affirmations is to integrate them into your daily routine. So set a reminder on your phone for a convenient time each day to read through and say your affirmations.

Take Action

1. Write down everything you want to accomplish in your life that's currently a big dream. Be very specific about what the dream is, down to the minute details. You should be able to tie each of these dreams to your financial goals.
2. Next, using the example affirmations I provided in this section, write down your own list of affirmations that you can repeat to yourself on a daily basis. Feel free to include your affirmations as part of your daily meditations or prayers.

Surround yourself only with people who are going to lift you higher.

– Oprah Winfrey

Who you associate with is who you become.

– Peter Voogd

SHIFT YOUR CIRCLE OF INFLUENCE

Several years ago, I read an article by a writer named Peter Voogd who wrote about what it takes to make six figures.[3] One of his steps to increase your earning potential was to shift your circle of influence. This has resonated with me ever since. Your circle of influence – the people you surround yourself with and take advice from – has a strong impact on how successful you become, especially when it comes to your finances.

Voogd writes:

> Once you get clear on who you are and what you want, you must re-evaluate your *Circle of Influence*. Who you associate with is who you become.. . .
>
> If you hang around five confident people, you will be the sixth.
>
> If you hang around five intelligent people, you will be the sixth.
>
> If you hang around five millionaires, you will be the sixth.
>
> If you hang around five idiots, you will be the sixth.
>
> If you hang around five broke people, you will be the sixth.
>
> It's inevitable.[4]

Simply said, you are the average of the five people you spend the most time with. Knowing this, it's important to understand just how your circle of influence impacts your financial goals.

[3]"Shifting Your Circle of Influence," https://www.entrepreneur.com/slideshow/306646#3.

[4]"Shifting Your Circle of Influence," https://www.entrepreneur.com/slideshow/306646#3.

The people and things you surround yourself with (including what you read, what you listen to, and what you watch) have a strong impact on your finances, whether you choose to believe it or not. If you are continuously surrounded by people who think they can never save, or they can never pay off debt and are all about accepting what life gives them, then you are very likely to start thinking the same way because there's nothing motivating or empowering you to do better.

If you are constantly around unambitious, unmotivated, YOLO-type people (e.g. Miss Ain't-Got-No-Goals) who only encourage you to spend, spend, and spend some more and who think attempting to build wealth is a waste of your time, then you're probably going to start thinking, "Yes, I live only once. Plus, everyone has debt anyway. . .it's normal."

If you are spending most of your time watching or reading things that add nothing to the progress you want to make with your finances, then it's the same – you'll find it harder to get the motivation you need to start making progress.

So how do you know when you need to make a shift? Well, it's actually not that difficult. You simply start by taking an assessment of the people and things around you as they relate to what you want to accomplish.

For example, if you've been thinking about and talking about paying off debt, but everyone around you is adopting a "Debt is normal" mentality, that's an indication that you need to shift your circle of influence.

If you've been wanting to start a business, but everyone around you thinks starting a business is a waste of time, that's another indication.

Think you can't find a better job that pays you more money because everyone is telling you it's impossible? It's time to make that shift.

Then you want to set a goal to find and surround yourself with people and things that are going to get you motivated to do better and that challenge you to actually start accomplishing your goals.

The bottom line is, you are more likely to accomplish your goals if you are surrounded with the right influences.

I know, I know. It sounds like I'm telling you to ditch your friends and family or start telling everyone off. But that's not what this is. Shifting your circle of influence doesn't mean you start picking fights or cutting people off for no reason. It means that once you identify the type of people you want to spend more time with, do that. You'll eventually spend less time with the people who have nothing to contribute to your purpose or progress.

It also doesn't mean that you'll never watch your favorite reality TV show again. Instead, it means cutting back the amount of time you spend watching TV so you can allocate time to doing more productive things like reading a personal finance blog or a personal development book. Rather than eliminating the non-productive, think of it as adding in opportunities for good.

I've personally had to shift my circle of influence several times in the past. For example, years ago when I was pursuing my first big savings goal (which I'll get into more in Chapter 3), I had friends who would make fun of my frugal ways and call me cheap, and when I first started my business, I had friends who didn't understand why I would want to pursue a business when I had a great job and a promising career path. They would make snide remarks and joke about what I was doing and were generally unsupportive. Each time I had to make a choice: to stop what I was doing so I could please others and fit in, or to focus on my goals regardless of what those friends said or thought about me.

I chose the latter because I wanted to achieve my goals badly enough and because I realized that perhaps I was outgrowing some friendships. And so I took a simple step to shift my circle of influence; I stopped talking to those people about my goals and what I was doing, and by doing this, they no longer had the opportunity to discourage me because I didn't give it to them.

Instead, I chose to share things only with supportive and like-minded friends pursuing similar goals. We motivated each other to keep going and kept ourselves accountable.

There was also a period where I've found myself falling down a rabbit hole of "woe is me" emotions and feeling completely demotivated when it came to my goals. After reflecting on why I was feeling this way, I found that I was spending way too time watching negative news. And so, to shift away from the influence the news was having on me, I decided to stop spending my time watching things I could not control (there will always be negative news) and instead I focused on getting more positive inputs into my life, such as waking up to pray and meditate each morning instead of immediately turning on the TV to watch the news or browse the media websites.

Shifting away from the people and things that don't serve your purpose or help you progress solves one of the problems. You can feel confident that you won't be isolating yourself or completely getting rid of things and people you like; instead, you are being more intentional about whom you share things with and what you spend your time on. But what about that other issue? What do you do if you don't already know people who share your goals and outlook on personal finance?

Thank goodness for the Internet! You can find virtual mentors online. If you really don't have anyone around you who motivates and positively influences you, turn to online communities. Identify a few people you admire who have achieved a goal you are trying to reach. Study them, read what they've written, watch interviews with them, and join their online communities. You'll find many other like-minded people there – and they can become your new circle of influence. I've met so many incredible people and made some great friends from online communities and some of my personal virtual mentors are Michelle Obama, Oprah Winfrey, Warren Buffett, and Sara Blakely.

Shifting your circle of influence will not just help you get and stay motivated, but you'll also have the opportunity to learn exactly how you can accomplish your goals from people who have already done what you are seeking to do. This, in turn, will change your mindset and your outlook on life, and impact your personal development and growth.

When it comes to shifting your circle of influence, be intentional about the relationships you cultivate and what you spend your time doing. Surround yourself with people who will motivate and support you. Be mindful of the content you consume and activities you partake in. Doing this will create room for the right people and things in your life and in turn will help you become the best version of yourself.

Take Action

Take an assessment of your current circle of influence and reflect on your answers:

- Whom are you spending your time with?
- Do your friends and acquaintances encourage your goals and dreams?
- Do they motivate you to expand and accomplish more, or do they hinder your progress?
- Are there any toxic relationships that you need to distance yourself from?
- What are you spending your free time doing?
- Are these activities aligned with your long-term goals and values?
- Do they contribute to your personal growth and development?
- Are there hobbies or interests you want to explore that could also have a positive impact on your life?
- What shifts do you need to make to help you get on track with your financial goals?

MEET LATOYA SCOTT

Latoya is a Certified Financial Education Instructor (CFEI) and a personal finance writer for her website http://lifeandabudget.com. She helps women and their families find financial freedom without resorting to coupon cutting or obsessing over credit scores.

On her journey to becoming debt free, Latoya has gone from feeling ashamed and depressed about money to rising above those feelings, breaking up with the paycheck-to-paycheck lifestyle, and becoming financially carefree, essentially having a life and a budget! Now she shares some of the money mistakes she's made and the valuable lessons she learned from them.

Some of your worst money mistakes were in college. What would you tell your younger self, knowing what you know now?

> Twelve years out of college and two kids later, I would let myself know that retail therapy does not heal my issues. For many years, I suppressed my emotional problems through shopping. My shopping addiction is gone now, and I have a much better emotional state of mind. Now, when I'm going through something, I have other tools to fall back on instead of pulling out my credit card for a shopping spree.
>
> These tools include meditation, writing, family, and reading. When I'm having stressful days, it's way more affordable to cozy up in bed with a good book. Reading is something I can do for hours and never get bored. The same with writing. I think it's about finding the things that bring you pure joy and doing these things without shame when the going gets tough.
>
> I would also definitely tell myself to prioritize increasing my cash flow through assets versus getting hooked on climbing the career ladder. A little

over a year ago, I was let go from a job I would have been at for 10 years. I'd grown tired of the work, so I wasn't sad to see it go, but I wish I would have utilized my time better while I was there and built some cash-flow assets instead of chasing job titles.

You've filed for bankruptcy in the past. What lessons did you learn from the experience?

I learned that credit cards can be easily abused when you don't have the emotional capacity and intellectual know-how to use them to your advantage.

I think having the intellectual know-how of the importance of saving money would have done wonders for me at such a young age. When I was younger, I saved all of my extra money in a cup behind my bed so that I would be able to purchase everyone (extended family included) Christmas presents. I was really young. . .second or third grade. I knew how to be a consumer, but I didn't know how to save for a better future.

My family didn't save money as a way to protect you from life. They might have saved to satisfy an immediate want (such as Christmas presents), but even then that didn't happen often. Credit cards were a way of life, and I didn't have the intellectual know-how to use credit cards to my advantage. Instead, I used them to purchase things I wanted but couldn't afford.

There are so many ways to earn cash-back rewards and make credit cards worth your while. But these are things I was incapable of taking advantage of at a certain point in my life.

Getting over these money mistakes requires forgiving yourself. How did you do it?

> You have to show yourself grace. Oftentimes, other people will forgive you for something long before you'll forgive yourself, and it can take an emotional toll on you. As long as you're living, there are mistakes to be made. And what I've learned is that they aren't really mistakes – they are lessons that are definitely worth your while if you take note and make an effort to actually learn something from them.

What is the most important thing that has led to your success with money now?

> The most important thing that has led to my success with money at this point in my life is knowing exactly what I want. When I was young, I was simply going through the motions. . .trying to survive one day to the next. Now, I know exactly what I want, and I'm getting it. It's very easy to be successful with money when you have the end in mind.
>
> Right now, I'm motivated to increase my income so I can pay off my debt more quickly, and I also want to build more passive streams of income.

CHAPTER 2

Get Organized

Visible mess helps distract us from the true source of the disorder.

– Marie Kondo

GET YOUR RECORDS IN ORDER

Before you create the master plan for your finances, you need to get things organized. Getting your finances organized will contribute to your financial success, because it's so much easier to execute and be successful with a plan when you know where everything is and have all the information you need whenever you need it. At the very minimum, you'll be able to find things easily, and you'll be aware of any gaps you need to fill or issues you need to address around your financial records. You'll need to organize your bank accounts, your financial (and other related) records, and your insurance records.

So let's talk through the details.

Bank Accounts

Bank accounts are where you process the majority of your daily transactions, including your savings and investments, so it's important that you have the right accounts set up for your needs. Here are a few types of accounts you can have in place that can help you keep your money organized:

- A bill payments account for day-to-day spending, to pay your household bills, and for debt repayment
- An emergency savings account
- A short- to mid-term savings account – for goals like buying a house or car, or saving for a vacation
- Retirement investment accounts
- Nonretirement investment accounts – like savings for your child's college education and other long-term goals
- Separate business checking and savings accounts if you are a business owner

Personally, I have bill payment accounts, multiple short-term savings accounts (I like to keep my savings for different short-term goals separate), retirement savings accounts, investment accounts for my children's college education, and business savings and checking accounts.

The actual number of accounts you have really depends on you. It's all about making sure you are able to keep track of where your money is and what it's for. If you don't have much to keep track of, you can use fewer accounts and track those amounts separately. It really comes down to personal preference for how many accounts you hold and how you organize your money. The point is that you are aware of where your money is, where it should be going, and what you've already allocated it to.

Financial Records

We live in a day and age where security breaches and identity theft are becoming all too common, unfortunately, and so your financial records (whether physical or electronic) and the details of each record (account numbers, beneficiary information, specific contact information) should be stored in a safe place like a home safe, or an encrypted folder on your computer or in an encrypted cloud account. These may include:

- Social Security cards
- Insurance policies
- Warranties
- Investment details
- Tax returns
- Loan documents
- Wills
- Nonfinancial records like diplomas and passports

The important thing is that you keep track of your records, know where everything is, and can access them when necessary. You may also want your partner, close relative, or lawyer to know where things are in the event that you need records but aren't available to get them yourself.

Insurance Records

The purpose of insurance is that it serves as your backup in the event of a serious situation. It means you won't have to derail your financial plans if something terrible happens. So, as part of this organization process, you'll want to review your insurance policies to make sure you have the right type of coverage for your individual life scenario and that you know where all the information is if you find you have to make a claim. At a minimum, your coverage should include:

- Auto insurance
- Health insurance
- Home or rental insurance
- Life insurance (if you have children or other people who depend on your income)
- Personal article insurance (if you own expensive jewelry, electronics, or other items)
- Disability insurance

You may not necessarily have all of these insurances at the moment, nor do you necessarily need all of them. The point here is to know what you do have and what you need, where your records are, and how you can make a claim if necessary. It also means you've updated your beneficiaries and figured out if there's any additional insurance you need.

How Long Should I Keep My Records?

Honestly, this is one of the most common questions I'm asked when organization comes up. Knowing how long to keep your records will allow you to have everything you need when you need it, while also keeping your records as streamlined as possible. This way, you're not sifting through anything that's no longer needed, yet you don't get rid of anything you'll likely need in the future.

Here is a quick overview of how long you should keep your various financial records:

Active accounts and obligations – keep while active

- Insurance documents
- Contracts
- Retirement plan contributions
- Equity and stock records
- Brokerage statements
- Home improvement records
- Property tax records
- Ongoing debt repayments
- Records for items associated with active warranties
- Records for items that have not exceeded their return dates

Records to keep permanently

- Birth certificates or adoption paperwork
- Death certificates
- Marriage certificates
- Wills
- Records of mortgages you've paid off on housing, land, and other property
- IRA contribution statements for nondeductible contributions

Records to keep at least seven years

- Tax returns
- Tax-related records (e.g. alimony payments, charitable contributions)

Records to keep at least three years

- Canceled insurance policies
- Property sales (e.g. investments and real estate)
- Paid medical bills
- Capital gains and losses reports, other deductions for your tax returns

Records to keep at least one year

- Canceled checks
- Paycheck records
- Bill payment records
- Bank statements

TIP

If you're thinking about tossing financial records, ask yourself if you still need them, if they're necessary for legal reasons, if they could be handy later, and if you have space for them. Also consider securely digitizing them for convenience and easy access.

Take Action

Get your financial records organized:

1. Make a list of all your financial records using the examples mentioned as a guide. This might take a little bit of time, so don't be in a hurry.
2. Locate your tax returns and any recurring statements you receive by physical mail or email. This includes statements for your utility or mortgage payments, credit cards, student loans, and bank and insurance statements.

3. Highlight the important information on them, like account numbers, contact phone numbers and addresses, interest rates, and so on.
4. Organize this information into an app with encryption capabilities, a spreadsheet, or a physical binder that you store securely.

Depending on how much information you have, this exercise could take some time, but that's okay! Once you've gotten everything organized, you'll be so glad you did. It will give you a better sense of the big picture of your finances and help you make decisions later on.

Your spending habits – not your salary – make you rich.

#CLEVERGIRLSKNOW

TRACK YOUR SPENDING

Have you ever felt like every time you get paid, your money conveniently finds ways to leave you? Like seriously, how annoying! Why can't those dollars just stay put? If it's not a random bill, it's a gift, something your kid wants, an impromptu night out with friends, that new dress. . .ugh.

Well, here's a not-so-secret secret – if you don't tell your money what to do, it will do whatever the heck it feels like doing. *#fact*

Allow me to illustrate. Think of your dollar bills as employees in a company called *you*. As CEO, you assign them their various job functions, which may include paying down debt, building your emergency fund, investing for retirement, and other goals required to build your empire. Having a solid business strategy in place will tie into how successful your company is. In this case, your business strategy is called – drumroll – your budget.

None of your employees should be allowed to sit around doing nothing to add value to your bottom line, otherwise they have a high chance of slipping away unaccounted for, and you'll find yourself wondering where they went after a while. Ever notice those employees at your job who always seem to be in the break room? Yeah, you don't want that happening at the company of *you*.

When it comes to keeping an eye on your money, one way to get into the flow of things is to actually keep track of where it's going. You can do this in one of several ways: by using an app that tracks your spending, with a spreadsheet, or with good old pen and paper in a notebook. Whichever method you choose, the key is to do it frequently and consistently. This way, you know exactly what's happening with your money.

The whole point of tracking your money is to be more aware of your spending, help you identify your spending habits, and help you identify areas for improvement. Tracking your spending can be an incredibly eye-opening exercise if you follow through.

Starting Out

To start out, at least for the first couple of weeks, I highly recommend a pen and notebook (a spending journal) that you carry around with you. Later, you can transition over to an app or even a simple spreadsheet.

Why? There's just something about putting pen to paper when you first start this exercise and seeing things laid out in your own handwriting that helps with perspective. Psychology, magic – call it what you will – it works!

In order to be successful in tracking your spending, you need to commit to writing down every single transaction you make every single day for those first two weeks. From a pack of gum to coffee to lunch, whether you used your debit card, spent cash, or used your credit card – every single transaction should go into your spending journal. You can either write down your transactions as they happen or collect all your receipts and document your transactions at the end of each day.

You want to add enough detail in your journal to allow you to review your spending at the end of the week. To make sure you remember what it was that you spent money on, consider including the following:

- The date
- The item description
- How much you spent
- What it was for and how you felt about it

You can also take things a step further by pulling out the last three months of your credit card and bank statements to take a look at how you've spent money historically. This can help you begin to piece together your spending patterns and provide a baseline for your analysis.

As part of this analysis, mark up your highest spending categories to determine where you've spent the most and where you see opportunities to scale back. Certain apps will do this for you automatically, but you can also use a highlighter in your journal to start out. Keep all of these insights in mind as you track your spending going forward.

 **TIP**

It's a good idea to track your spending as part of your normal routine. This will eliminate any overwhelm with the process. If you are tracking your spending for the very first time (or the first time in a long time), set daily reminders on your phone and don't forget to get a copy of each receipt so you don't forget anything.

Reviewing Your Spending Journal

As you make progress with tracking your spending, plan to review what you are tracking at least once a week to see how you're doing. Remember, the goal is to help you gain clarity around your spending habits, so don't judge yourself too harshly.

Instead, come up with a plan or steps to adjust your spending patterns or habits as you start to identify them. Then build the changes into your budget.

As you track, you'll start to find that you are more aware of your spending habits, and you will even start to make better decisions around your money. That's because now you're actively thinking things through as opposed to spending money without giving it much thought. You may also find that you are spending less, which is the perfect opportunity to use those freed-up funds toward your debt repayment or savings.

After all is said and done, it's definitely a worthwhile exercise!

Take Action

Review and track your spending:

1. Determine exactly how you plan to track your spending – with a pen and notebook (I highly recommend this for the first two weeks), with a spreadsheet, or by choosing an app to automate the tracking process.
2. Pull out your bank and credit card statements for the last three months and go over your spending history to start identifying your spending habits. Based on this review, break your spending out into categories, see what you spent where, and determine where you can cut back and by how much.
3. Set a daily reminder to spend five minutes going over your spending for each day. (If you don't spend anything on a particular day, celebrate with a happy dance!)
4. Set a weekly reminder for 15–30 minutes to review things in more detail at the end of each week.

The chains of habit are too light to be felt until they are too heavy to be broken.

– Warren Buffett

#CLEVERGIRLSKNOW

IDENTIFY YOUR BAD MONEY HABITS

We are all guilty of having one bad habit or another. It could be spending countless hours on social media instead of getting work done, watching way too much reality TV, or spending money on unnecessary stuff.

Personally, one of my bad habits is checking my phone. All the time. Thank you, social media. I'm seriously working on this, though, and while it can be really hard to do sometimes, I know that getting a handle on it will help me be less distracted with my work and in my personal life. It's a bad habit worth breaking, and while bad habits have different levels of severity, some of the worst habits are based on money and spending – they impact your entire life.

The problem is that habits are just incredibly hard to break. Often, we start up a habit slowly, like overspending, without even realizing it's happening. Then several months pass and you've gone way over budget. Now you try to stop the spending, but it's become a part of your routine – breaking it becomes a serious challenge. I'll give you a simple yet common example.

Let's say you stop by a coffee shop one day and they have such incredible coffee, and even though it's more expensive than the other coffee shops you go to, you find yourself back there the next day and then the next day and then all of a sudden it becomes your new favorite coffee shop. Every morning, as if on autopilot, you stop by to get some coffee and perhaps even a yummy pastry every now and then.

Then one day, you decide you are going to stop because it's way too expensive and you want to save some money.

Well, the next time you drive by that favorite coffee shop of yours, you'll probably be just fine sticking to your guns. But as you drive by a few more times, you'll probably have a mental battle with yourself – you'll rationalize why you deserve it, how you need your coffee buzz, how the cheaper coffee at the other shops you know doesn't compare, how the coffee at work is terrible, oh, and there's the amazing smell. . . .

And then perhaps you'll start some self-negotiation and tell yourself, "It will only be for today," or "I'll start skipping the coffee shop every other day." Maybe you'll even convince yourself that this is a super-stressful week, so you'll just plan to stop going there next week. Or maybe next month. . .

See what I mean about habits being hard to break?

I'm absolutely not saying that you can't have your fancy coffee. You actually should be able to splurge on life's little pleasures, but the important thing to keep in mind is that splurging can easily turn into a habit, which can become hard to break. The last thing you want is for your bad habit to be responsible for ruining your potential financial success.

I'm not saying buying coffee could potentially ruin you (well, it could if you are buying the entire store out every day, but I digress). What I'm saying is that all bad habits work this way – it starts with one or two splurges and becomes a daily or weekly spend. Insert any bad money habit into this example above and you'll find that things play out in a similar fashion.

Some of the most common bad money habits include:

- Overspending
- Not creating a monthly budget
- Paying your bills late
- Carrying a credit card balance that you don't pay in full each month, even when you have the cash to do so
- Using your emergency fund for things that are not emergencies (Ahem, coffee and manicures are not emergencies.)
- Not saving because you think you don't earn enough
- Not investing because you think you are too young, too old, it's too complicated, or you'll just figure it out later
- Paying for subscription services that you never use

Do any of the above sound familiar? Can you relate to scenarios where you find yourself committing these bad habit offenses time and time again?

Bad habits are pretty easy to start but very hard to break. As the great Warren Buffett once said, "The chains of habit are too light to be felt until they are too heavy to be broken."

According to researchers from University College London, it takes an average of 66 days to break a bad habit.[1] It's also much harder to stop doing something without replacing that behavior. So, if you are trying to break a bad money habit or two, it would be much easier if you:

1. First identify each of your bad money habits, including where you find yourself doing them and the feelings that trigger them.
2. Plan out in advance what actions you can take to replace the habit or actions that trigger the habit. With the coffee example, for instance, you could:
   - Take a different route to work so you don't have the reminder.
   - Brew your own coffee at home so you don't have an excuse to buy it.
   - Leave your credit card at home.
   - Choose to leave cash at home or in the bank so you can't pay to feed your habit.

One important thing to know as you work on breaking your bad money habits is that sometimes our habits can come from various money myths (aka lies about money) that we have somehow come to believe. They could be ideas we have been raised with or ideas that have been impressed upon us by people we interact with or even ideas that come from content we consume on a frequent basis.

---

[1] *How Are Habits Formed: Modelling Habit Formation in the Real World,* http://repositorio.ispa.pt/bitstream/10400.12/3364/1/IJSP_998-1009.pdf

And when we start believing a myth, it can influence our financial behaviors and cause us to adopt negative attitudes toward money or feel like we can never accomplish our goals. Many times, these beliefs can lead to poor decision-making and bad habits like overspending, avoiding saving or investing, accumulating debt, and neglecting our overall financial wellness.

So it's important that you identify any money myths you currently believe and start dispelling them immediately. Here are some common, widespread money beliefs and why they are not true:

Money myth #1: Money is the root of all evil.

This is one of the most popular money myths out there. And while the statement may be true to a degree, it is often misconstrued. The original statement comes from the Bible: "*For the love of money* is the root of evil." And this is because money itself is not evil; it is simply a tool that can be used for evil *or* for good, depending on the holder. If someone has evil intentions, access to money can make it easier to act on those evil intentions. The same applies to someone who has good intentions, where money can be used to create positive impact and change.

Believing that money is evil can have a significant impact on your attitude and behavior toward money. You might develop a negative mindset toward building wealth and think of it as greedy. This belief can also sabotage your ability to achieve financial success because you may actively avoid saving or investing, which in turn can lead to a lack mentality and financial stress.

Again, money is simply a tool, and having it can create incredible positive change for you, your family, and even your community at large.

Money myth #2: You need a lot of money to invest.

Investing to build wealth is not just for the rich. In fact, most people who have built wealth without an inheritance or a handout have done so by starting small and investing consistently over time. Don't let this myth make you fall into the habit of not investing.

So many online platforms today will allow you to invest in the stock market on a fractional basis with small amounts of money, as little as $1 to $10. There are also several low-cost investment options for index funds, exchange-traded funds (ETFs), real estate investment trusts (REITs), bond funds, and more, which make investing accessible at different income levels.

So the idea that you need a lot of money to invest in today's world is false, and starting small can still help you build long-term wealth as long as you stay consistent and invest smartly. (We'll discuss more on investing in Chapter 5.) The money you save by avoiding the expensive coffee store from my earlier example (or insert whatever habit you want to break – maybe buying fast fashion *cough* Shein, eating out every day, etc.) can add up quickly and this is money you can start investing!

Money myth #3: Personal finance is hard, so leave it to the professionals.

This is another myth that is far from the truth and one that causes people to fall into the habit of neglecting their overall financial wellness. But it is not surprising, because money can be intimidating. That said, you do not need to be a financial expert or hire a financial professional to effectively manage your money without fear.

The key to tackling feeling intimidated about money is to increase your financial knowledge (high five – you're doing that just by reading this book!) and apply what you learn to create your financial plans and adjust them as necessary, when necessary.

There are so many resources available to help you to learn more about money and increase your financial knowledge, including our free courses at Clever Girl Finance, books like this one (and the rest of the Clever Girl Finance series), podcasts, apps, online communities, and more.

Money myth #4: It's not polite to talk about money.

This entire book dispels that myth because that's just what we're doing – talking about money! So many of us have the habit of avoiding money conversations.

There is this idea that money is a taboo topic and it's not polite to discuss. What this does is discourage open discussions about money. But if done the right way, talking about money can in fact be informational, healthy, motivating, and empowering.

The many money conversations I've had have taught me so much, from how to ask for a raise when I worked in corporate America, to exploring different ideas on budgeting, to getting motivation to save and invest, to starting my own business, to getting talked out of even more money mistakes I could have made along the way. All those conversations have been instrumental on my wealth-building journey.

Additionally, talking about money can help to eliminate the stigma people feel about being open about their financial mistakes and struggles. Talking with the right people about your money concerns (e.g. nonjudgmental friends and family, financial professionals, and even therapists) can provide the support you need to better navigate financial challenges.

Money myth #5: Getting your finances in order is punishment.

A lie! On the contrary, getting your finances together is for your benefit, and not just for your current self but for your future self too. You are setting the stage to create options for yourself so you can live a life on your own terms, not one dictated by a lack of savings or a ton of debt.

It also doesn't mean you can't live a good life or enjoy yourself while you get your finances in order. There are so many ways in which you can live a full life and have fun. Examples include budget-friendly outings, taking advantage of free events, potluck parties, preplanned trips, starting a passion project or side hustle you enjoy, and more – no punishment involved!

These are just a few money myths that can fuel bad money habits. The good news is that with concentrated effort and consistency, it gets easier to break your bad habits over time. That being said, it's important to identify what those bad habits are now, as well as any money myths you've come to believe, so you know which specific areas you need to focus on. This way, you can go from being your own worst financial enemy to being your best advocate for your financial success.

Take Action

Work on the following exercise to help you curb your bad money habits:

1. Make a list of every single bad money habit you have that comes to mind, organized by level of severity or impact on your finances. Not sure what they are? Go over your credit card and bank statements and review your spending.
2. For each habit, write down the triggers (including time and place) or the behaviors that cause you to engage in this habit. If you're not sure, monitor yourself. When you catch yourself thinking about or doing that habit, take note of how you're feeling and what led you there.
3. Assess if your habits and triggers are associated with any money myths you might believe. Make a note of what the myth is and then write down why that myth is a lie!
4. Next, come up with an alternative action that you can take when this trigger happens. Perhaps you change your route to work, avoid certain stores, keep cash at home – whatever it is, try to do this consistently to help yourself, rather than leaving it up to willpower.
5. Finally, determine a reward you can give yourself if you are able to stay consistent with breaking your habit. For example, if you stay away from the coffee shop for a month, maybe treat yourself to a cup. Or maybe you buy yourself a fancy coffee machine for your home (that you've planned for in your budget).

MEET CHRISTINA MYCHAS

Christina creates life and style content on her YouTube channel, *Minimalist-ish* (http://YouTube.com/@ChristinaMychas), and is the co-host of the podcast *Sustain This!* She is a reformed shopaholic turned intentional spender, who now helps others find inner motivation to become content with what they have and who they are by focusing on curation over clutter.

Christina successfully adjusted her money habits to overcome a shopping addiction and pay off over $120,000 of debt. She shares her journey to overcoming that addiction by breaking up with her bad habits and ditching the money myths that were holding her back.

Can you describe the specific money habits that contributed to your shopping addiction and where they came from?

> I had a chronic urge to spend money and I think that came from boredom, anxiety, loneliness, and a lack of control. I felt like the way I could get control back was by controlling my appearance and my personal style.
>
> At the time I was working full-time and making more money than I'd ever made in my life, and at the same time I was watching my peers go on trips, buy new cars, and buy new homes. And so, in my mind, I had to keep up with a certain level of affluence among my peers because I am a pharmacist.
>
> I liked to keep up through fashion and shopping because it gave me a sense of control that I felt was lacking. I thought that if I could control my appearance and how people perceived me, I could hide the fact that I was out of control with my money.
>
> As a result, I would impulse-buy things; I would see an item, like it, and just buy it. I would watch YouTube haul videos where influencers linked to different items with affiliate links, and I would follow these influencers and shop their links. It was exciting that I could use the same bronzer or highlighter that my favorite influencer used because at the time, to me, they were almost like celebrities, and it made me feel like I was on a similar level because I could buy the same things they did.

How did your bad money habits impact your financial situation or goals?

Well, I was broke. I was making over six figures pretty much straight out of school, and I spent it all. I blamed a lot of things other than my shopping for being broke. For instance, I blamed my student loans. I had $120,000 of student loan debt and my monthly minimum payment was $1200. I was also living alone in Toronto, which is an expensive city with a high cost of living. And while I could make my minimum payments and I could pay my rent, the rest of my money was just wasted on stuff.

I also couldn't make any progress on my loan. I remember looking at my loan one day and thinking I had paid off $12,000 to $15,000 that year, but then I saw that only $5000 went to my principal balance and I just told myself I was going to be in debt forever, I wasn't going to be able to do anything that I wanted to do, and money was always going to be a stressor because of my impulse buying and lack of control with my money.

Were there any specific money myths you believed that kept you in debt?

The money myths I believed were that I couldn't be good with money, and I wasn't a person who could learn about money because I wasn't a finance person. This thinking kept me in a victim mindset for a long time.

One of the big steps you took to address your spending habits was to start a low-buy year. How did this help you address your habits?

Doing a low-buy year transformed my life. It allowed me to detox and give myself space to change my relationship with my money, my shopping, and my stuff; I had a closet full of clothes bursting at the seams. A lot of people spend their money either in their fridges or in their closets. For me, it was my closet.

First, I did a no-buy for about six months and then after that I transitioned to a low-buy. I did this because as much as you may want to go cold turkey to change your habits, true habit change takes time. It's kind of like when you start going to the gym or working out, you're not going to see abs right away. Instead, it's showing up to change your habits and voting for that new goal or identity every single time you show up and that just takes time. So for me personally, this approach really helped.

You went on to pay off over $120,000 of debt. How did you stay motivated and disciplined while working to change your habits?

I think I was able to stay motivated and disciplined because I saw the light at the end of the tunnel, and over time I could see my debt going down with every extra payment I made.

I loved seeing my debt go down and I loved finding ways to gamify it. Like if I cut something out of my spending, then I could put even more toward my debt. I was just so mad at my debt that it caused tunnel vision and that really kept me focused.

Did you face any challenges or setbacks along the way? How did you overcome them?

My debt payoff was very much a slow-and-steady thing, but I relapsed into old shopping and impulse-buying behaviors during my journey, especially in that first year.

As I mentioned, my no-buy lasted about six months and within that timeframe, my family dog passed away, which was very sudden and unexpected. He was the love of my life and so I leaned back into old habits to cope, and I learned that I dealt with my stress, sorrow, and anxiety by shopping. That was when I transitioned to a low-buy year.

I also got to know myself more and had to deal with all the different mindsets, assumptions, and limiting beliefs I had about myself and about money in general. I had to work through my financial trauma and my self-esteem along the way and really get clear about the life I could shape for myself if my money was my own.

I overcame these challenges by staying consistent with paying off my debt, which I did. And I proved to myself that if I kept going and stayed consistent, I could do it. This was huge in terms of building my self-confidence and getting clear on what I really wanted, versus staying stuck and doing the same things over and over.

How do you maintain your improved money habits now?

I still budget every single day and I track my spending, but now I can be a little freer with my money because I am debt free and I'm living on the other side of all the things I was dreaming of when I set out to get out of debt.

Now that I have freed up more money, to avoid falling back into my old habits, I have a wish list for the things I want to buy, and I have a "fun money" budget and a "guilt-free spending" budget that I do my best to stick to.

I refuse to let myself get into debt for anything ever again. It's just not worth it and I don't want to have to go through that journey again.

Knowing where you stand financially will help you make plans to get where you want to go.

#CLEVERGIRLSKNOW

KNOW YOUR NET WORTH

Once you've gotten things organized and started to work on breaking those bad money habits, you're ready to get into the details. Let's find out your net worth – cue the drumroll and the marching band! I love tracking my net worth, and you should, too!

Why all the excitement? Well, your net worth is an indicator of the progress you're making. No matter how small it might seem sometimes, especially when compared to the big picture, progress is progress. And consistent progress gets you closer to your financial goals!

Tracking your net worth will show you what kind of progress you're making and help you see that your small changes impact the big picture. Your net worth shows you where you stand financially and helps you create a plan of attack to get your numbers up.

However, calculating and tracking net worth can be a touchy subject. While some people love doing it, others might hate facing the reality of what their net worth might be at the current moment. Notice my emphasis on "current moment" here. Remember, where you are right now is only temporary, and you are now taking the steps to make real progress on improving things. After all, that's why you are reading this book, right?

So let's work those numbers out.

How to Calculate Your Net Worth

Well, it's pretty straightforward. Your net worth is calculated by subtracting your liabilities from your assets.

$$\text{Net worth} = \text{Assets}(\text{what you own}) - \text{Liabilities}(\text{what you owe})$$

Yup, that's it. It's basically taking the value of all the things you owe (mortgages, credit card debt, student loans, car loans, etc.) from the value of all the things you own (real estate, vehicles, cash, investments, jewelry, etc.).

So let's say, for example, you own your own home and have a bit of retirement savings, but also have a mortgage, student loans, and credit card debt, then your net worth calculation would be the total value of your home and retirement accounts minus the value of your mortgage, student loans, and credit card debt.

Here's an example.

Your assets (what you own):
■ The value of your house and any other real estate you might own ■ The sum of your retirement savings ■ The sum in your bank accounts
MINUS (−) Your liabilities (what you owe): ■ The balance on your mortgage ■ The balance on your student loans ■ Your total credit card debt
EQUALS (=) Your net worth (as of the specified date)

If your net worth is negative, don't panic!

Many people start out with a negative net worth. If this is you, it's okay. A negative net worth usually occurs when you haven't earned enough or invested enough of your income to offset your debt. For example, it is not uncommon for younger people who have student loans to have a negative net worth because they typically haven't earned much at the beginning of their career.

Another reason for a negative net worth could be overspending and having large amounts of credit card debt without many assets to offset them. Given time and the continuous practice of good financial habits, this can change.

TIP

Feeling down about your current net worth? Shift your focus to actionable steps you can take for improvement, celebrate your wins as you make progress, lean on supportive friends and/or family, and be kind to yourself – it's a journey and you'll get there!

How to Increase Your Net Worth

Every time you make a payment toward debt or you put money in your savings account, you are increasing your net worth.

Even if it still remains negative, when you make a debt payment you are reducing the total amount of debt you carry, which in turn increases your net worth and will gradually move you out of the negative (the red) and into the positive (the black).

Some impactful moves you can take to increase your net worth could include:

- Increasing the amount you pay toward your debts each month. (We'll get into dealing with your debt in the next few chapters.)
- Acquiring more long-term investments to increase your assets. Investing in your retirement plan is a great example of this. Additionally, you can also invest outside of retirement in things like stocks, bonds, or real estate that have the potential for growth.
- Finding ways to reduce your expenses and increase your income so you can put more money toward paying down debt and saving or investing more.
- Reviewing your financial goals and progress on a regular basis, so you can make adjustments as needed to stay on track toward increasing your net worth.

Ultimately, increasing your net worth is just a matter of time and focused effort.

Take Action

Work on calculating your net worth:

1. Make a list of all your assets – the things you own.
2. Make a list of all your liabilities – what you owe.
3. Subtract your liabilities from your assets to get your net worth.
4. Make note of today's date and then set a reminder to repeat this exercise every quarter so you can track the progress you make as you take action toward your financial goals.

MEET BRITTNEY SUTTLE

Brittney is a CPA and money expert who offers financial services for female entrepreneurs at http://kniesandco.com, helping them earn more, save more, and pay themselves more. She's increased her net worth over the last several years and shares with us how she did it.

You've been steadily increasing your net worth over the last few years. What was the trigger that caused you to make this a focal point of your finances?

> Reading *Rich Dad, Poor Dad* after I graduated really changed my mindset on how I viewed money and wealth. Even as a college student, I associated "rich" with someone who had a big house, a nice car, and some great clothes. The book shifted my outlook on what wealth really looks like – and what it looks like is freedom. So, at 24, I decided that instead of trying to chase an idea that would only lead to more

stress (and years I would have to work), I decided to chase one that would allow me to live the life I truly wanted to live.

As your net worth goes up with each passing year, how has your relationship with money changed?

It's funny because now I almost think of increasing my net worth as a challenge, which is completely opposite of how I had thought about money previously. I used to think money was a tool for consuming – to travel, buy groceries, have a great night out with my ladies – but now I find that I'm trying to use it as a tool to grow my wealth and net worth. So instead of taking away from my freedom by spending it, I'm now using my money to add to it, and it's been such a fun process trying to figure out different ways to do so. In a sense, it's become a game – one that I love playing.

What advice would you give your younger self about the freedom that money gives you?

I would tell her to have a "Come to Jesus" meeting and really decide what she wants out of life, not blindly follow what everyone else tells her it should be. So many of us go down paths that others have set up just because it's the norm, but the fun in life comes from taking risks. Even if they don't pan out, major growth happens in those moments, which still makes them worth it. Don't be held back by failure – just chase those dreams, girl. And can I also say, invest in rental properties sooner?

Plan for what makes you happy!

#CLEVERGIRLSKNOW

DEFINE YOUR VALUES

At this point in the book, you should know where you stand with your finances, the lessons you've learned from your past money mistakes, what your big financial dreams are, and with whom you need to surround yourself.

Now, it's time to set some fresh financial goals.

Your financial goals are essentially the big picture of where you want to get with your finances. They are what you are working so hard to achieve – this is *your* dream, so you have to be clear on these goals. Once you know what they are, you can eliminate all the noise and focus on not just achieving your goals but knocking them out of the park.

However, in order to set financial goals that matter in your life, you need to determine your core values first.

Defining Your Core Values

Your core values are the things in life that are most important to you. In other words, these are the things you hold onto above all else. To be able to live the life of your dreams, you need to know what's most important to you in your life and prioritize these things accordingly. When your goals are structured around the things that really matter to you, you are more compelled to actually do what it takes to achieve them.

Defining your core values is a personal thing. What's most important to me might be completely different from what's most important to you, so when you work on defining your values, don't worry about what other people are doing. Instead, focus on what you really want and, most importantly, what will make you happy.

Typically, people's core values revolve around experiences, financial security, giving back, and their loved ones. For instance, if one of your dreams is to become a world traveler, exploring new cultures and different destinations, then one of your core values is *experience*.

If you want to build long-term wealth for you and your family so you can afford the nicer things in life and have peace of mind about money, then one of your core values is *financial security.*

If you want to build a school for less privileged children or give back to single mothers in need, then a core value of yours is *giving back.*

Not sure how to identify your core values? One exercise I love to do with people that really gets them thinking is what I call the Million-Dollar Game. Here's how it works.

All you need is a timer, a piece of paper, and a pen. In 10 minutes, I want you to write down what you'd do if I gave you $1 million, tax free with no strings attached. Once you're finished, take a look at the list – what did you choose to spend money on? Was it a luxury lifestyle? An experience? Charity? Or did you invest or save it? This exercise usually gets things flowing when it comes to outlining what really matters to you.

Once you've gone through the exercise of identifying your core values, you then want to prioritize them in the order in which you'd like to achieve them. Once you've done that, you'll have a solid foundation to build your financial goals on.

Take Action

Grab your pen and paper and play the Million-Dollar Game:

1. Set your timer to 10 minutes and write down what you'd do if I gave you $1 million with no strings attached. You can make a list, draw, or scribble – there is no order to how it should be done. There are no rules.
2. As you do the exercise, tap into your daydreams about how you imagine your life would be if money was no object, not worrying about what other people are thinking or doing.
3. Once the timer is up, organize your notes into a list in order of priority and tie each priority to a value: experiences, loved ones, financial security, giving back, and so on.

SET YOUR GOALS

Now that you know what you value and where you really want to be in life, let's talk about goals – specifically, your financial goals. Your financial goals are essentially the objectives you want to achieve with money based on the type of life you want to live or the future financial needs you will have.

Having solid financial goals in place gives you something specific to work toward, which in turn makes you more likely to achieve your objectives. In other words, having financial goals will set you on the path toward your financial success. It's one of the things that will help you tell your money where it needs to go.

Personally, having clear financial goals has been a major contributor to the success I've had with my finances. My goals have kept me focused and grounded even when I've veered off course. Having those goals reminds me of the big picture of what I want to accomplish with my money. That way, I'm able to get myself back on track.

Think about anything you've ever wanted to accomplish in your life that you committed to working on. It was probably tied to a goal linked to a desired result or end state that you wanted to have. The same applies to your financial goals. Having clear goals can keep you on track when it comes to paying off debt, managing your spending, saving money, and investing.

As you start to think of your financial goals, you should use your core values as a baseline. You also want to ensure the goals you create are specific and measurable, and based on the values and priorities you set in the last chapter. It also often helps to break your goals down into short-, mid-, and long-term ones.

Your Short-Term Goals

Short-term goals are the ones you want to accomplish within the next five years. So, for example, if debt freedom is at the top of your core values list and you want to pay off all your credit card debt within five years, then you would add this to your list of short-term goals.

To make it specific and measurable, you'll need to determine how much you owe in total and figure out how much you can afford to pay down each month in order for you to become debt free by a certain date. This is where the organization phase comes in. This information should be in your notes or records.

Based on your specific situation, your goal might look something like "Pay $500 a month toward my credit card debt in order to become debt free in the next 36 months."

Your Mid-Term Goals

Mid-term goals are the goals you want to accomplish in the next 5–10 years. So if homeownership is on your core values list, then saving up money for a down payment on a house might be at the top of your mid-term goal list. To make it specific, add details of how much you will save and for how long. It might look something like "Save $500 a month for the next 72 months for a $36,000 (10%) down payment on our first home."

Your Long-Term Goals

Long-term goals are the ones you want to accomplish 10–15 (or more) years from now. For instance, if financial security is top on your core values list, then an example of a long-term financial goal might be to start saving for your retirement. Your goal might be something like "Max out my annual 401(k) and target-date retirement fund contributions each year in order to amass $1,000,000 to retire comfortably in 30 years."

Taking your short-, mid-, and long-term goals into account, your financial goal list and priorities might look something like this:

My Financial Goals

Priority 1. Become debt free: Pay $500 a month toward my credit card debt in order to become debt free in the next 36 months (short-term goal).

Priority 2. Purchase our first home: Save $500 a month for the next 72 months for a $36,000 (10%) down payment on our first home (mid-term goal).

Priority 3. Retire in 30 years: Max out my annual 401(k) and target-date retirement fund contributions each year in order to amass $1,000,000 to retire comfortably (long-term goal).

Once you've outlined your goals, you can then build them into your budget and start tracking your progress on a monthly, quarterly, and annual basis. The goals would also directly tie into improving your net worth.

Take Action

Work on laying out your financial goals:

1. Go over your core values. What are the things that are most important to you in your life?
2. What would you like to achieve in the next 5, 10, and 15-plus years? Stick to three to five major financial goals.
3. Prioritize your goals out into short-term (less than 5 years), mid-term (5–10 years), and long-term (10-plus years) goals.
4. Determine the dollar amount for each of your goals, and write them out specifically. You'll then need to build line items in your budget to save and invest toward each goal each time you get paid. (We discuss budgeting in the next chapter.)
5. As your finances change, reevaluate your goals. If you get a raise or find a better-paying job, you might be able to increase your contributions to each goal or add new ones.

MEET MOLLY STILLMAN

Molly is a life and style blogger over at http://StillBeingMolly.com and the host of the podcast *Business with Purpose*. Her true passion lies in helping inspire women to know that they were created on purpose, with a purpose, and for a purpose. Identifying her own purpose is what began her journey out of debt and into financial freedom. Molly dug herself out of thousands of dollars in debt slowly but surely and has not looked back ever since.

It took getting to the lowest point of your life to finally come around and face your finances head on. What happened and why was this change necessary?

> I was a year out of college, making $30,000 a year as a high school teacher, and suddenly found myself a little over $36,000 in debt. I couldn't even make the minimum payments on my cards anymore. When I realized I was in more debt than I even made in a year, I had a panic attack and knew that I had to make a change. So I made the decision that day to change my financial situation, no matter how hard it was going to be.

You talk about paying off $36,000 in debt. How long did it take you and what was it like going through that journey day to day? What did it feel like after all that debt was gone?

> It took me almost four years to pay off the debt. The journey was long and brutal, but I knew I had to remain patient. I didn't get into debt overnight, so I knew I wasn't going to get out of it overnight. It took a ton of sacrifice – I had to cut back in a lot of areas and I had to have a lot of hard conversations with myself. There were days when I wanted to give

up and throw in the towel, but I didn't and I'm so grateful for that.

When the debt was gone, there was a huge weight lifted off, but in some ways, it wasn't as monumental as I'd hoped. It was kind of anticlimactic because even after the debt was gone, my lifestyle had already changed so drastically. Once my debt payments went away, instead of going back to my old lifestyle, I began to take the money I was spending on paying down my debt and put it into savings.

The emotions around money can be super-challenging. How did you master this challenge to come out on the other side of your financial situation debt free?

For me, personally, it was all about surrendering my finances and being a good steward of what I've been entrusted with. Now I look forward to saving and giving. I get excited about making important financial decisions that could positively impact my family and my community. Sure, money can still be stressful and emotional at times, but overall, I'd say that knowing that money is something I get to handle responsibly is a privilege.

What did walking this journey to debt freedom teach you about your mindset and what you are capable of?

It really taught me that I am capable of far more than I could ever imagine. I was so scared and so stressed, and I worked so hard. Getting out of debt was one of the most stressful and emotionally taxing things I've ever done. However, it made me smarter and stronger in the end. I'm so grateful for the journey I had to go through! Mistakes teach us so much about ourselves and about life.

What do you have in place financially to ensure you never get back into debt again?

> Thankfully, I'm married to a financial advisor who definitely would never let us get into debt! But in all seriousness, having a monthly budget that we stick to is our biggest saving grace. We don't allow ourselves to slip and let spending get out of control. It's been a complete lifestyle and mindset shift.

PART II
The Plan

Clever girls know . . . Failing to plan = planning to fail.

#CLEVERGIRLSKNOW

CHAPTER 3

Budgeting

It's not about how much money you make; it's about what you do with what you have.

#CLEVERGIRLSKNOW

BUDGETING 101: THE BASICS

Now let's talk about – drumroll, please – budgeting!

Budgeting is pretty much the most talked-about topic when it comes to getting your finances in order. It's essentially the foundation of financial wellness, so you've probably heard time and time again that you should budget. But what really happens when you don't?

Every so often, I talk with women who can't figure out where their money is going each month. It just somehow seems to slip away conveniently. A coffee here, a nail appointment there, dinner with friends, that new dress, a gift for your friend, that bill you forgot was coming. . .and then all of a sudden, you are several days away from your next paycheck, trying to stay afloat and tapping into the available balance on your credit card.

That's along the lines of what typically happens when you don't budget.

It's important to understand that having a budget of some form is truly important for your financial success. Your budget tells your money what to do – not the other way around. When you manage your money with a budget, every cent is accounted for, and you have full control over how much you spend and how much you save. You see, you are the boss of your money and you work way too hard for it to let it just slip through your fingers.

I personally prefer the word *plan* to the word *budget* because it doesn't sound so constraining. So if it helps, instead of your calling your outline for where your money goes a boring old budget, call it something you like that you'd be happy to do – or at the very least happy about your budget-naming skills. What about one of these?

- My fabulous money plan
- My plan to riches
- The death to debt plan

Basically, call it something you like that will motivate the heck out of you every time you think about it.

It also really helps when you look at your money objectively for what it really is – a tool to help you get the things you truly desire in life. That being said, here are a few tips to be successful with budgeting:

1. *Create a budget in advance of each month.* Creating a budget in advance of each month means that once the month starts, you have a plan and you aren't scrambling trying to figure out what to do. Plan to create your budget a few days before the month starts. This way, you have time to lay things out and figure out what your finances will look like in the upcoming month.
2. *Don't assume every month will be the same.* Every single month should be planned separately. No two months will be exactly the same financially, so you want to prepare in advance for things like one-off bills and one-time expenses, travel plans, or events you have to attend.
3. *Base your budget on your projected income for that month.* If you get paid once a month, twice a month, or every two weeks, base your budget on that projected income so you know exactly how much you have to budget. Keep in mind that if you get paid every two weeks, there will be months where you get three paychecks.
4. *Pay your expenses before splurging.* This means paying for your essentials, debts, and goals (savings and investments) first before you do any splurging or miscellaneous spending. The last thing you want is to find that you have overspent on what isn't necessary and don't have a way to pay your bills.
5. *Track your transactions.* Tracking your transactions allows you to make sure you stay within your budget and keeps you conscious of your spending habits. You can track your transactions in a spending journal, a spreadsheet, or with an automated app or online tool.

6. *Practice makes perfect.* Think of budgeting like riding a bike. You are going to fall off a few times, maybe even bruise your knee, but to master riding that bike, you'll need to get up each time and keep going. The same thing applies to your budget. It might not be perfect every month, but if you keep working at it, you can get pretty close and it will make all the difference when it comes to managing your money!

SETTING UP YOUR BUDGET USING CATEGORIES

In order to budget successfully, you need to understand where your money goes each month. So if you haven't already completed the action steps in the "Track Your Spending" section of this book, I strongly recommend that you do. At the very least, get a general idea of where your money is going – pull out your bank and credit card statements for the last three months and go over them in detail.

Organize your spending into categories and add up all the numbers by month. This will be a huge eye-opener as to where you are spending your money and on what.

You can break your monthly budget down into the following four categories:

1. **Money for Your Future Self and Your Emergency Fund**

   Ever heard the saying "Pay yourself first"? This should be a consistent part of any plan you make. Before you pay any bills or do any shopping, a portion of your earnings should be diverted into your retirement account for your future self and your emergency savings accounts for a rainy day. No ifs, no maybes. Just do it.

   Time goes by so quickly, and planning for the future version of you will ensure that you can enjoy your retirement and not have to depend on the government or your children to take care of you. Having an emergency fund will provide you with a buffer in the event of unforeseen problems. You can rely on your emergency savings instead of a credit card or other debt to pay off something that comes up unexpectedly.

Included in this category (or as a subcategory) should be money to pay off any debt you have. It's essential that you pay off your debt as soon as you can so you can shift your focus to building long-term wealth.

2. **Your Essentials**

   Next would be your essentials and needs – the things you need to live your life. This does not include money for shopping or getting your nails done; those are not essentials (neither are they emergencies). This is for things like your housing costs (mortgage or rent), transportation, and food.

3. **Your Other Financial and Life Goals**

   This would include money you are saving outside of your retirement account – your mid-term and long-term savings and investments, for instance, or saving for a home purchase or your kids' college.

4. **Everything Else**

   This is where your splurge money would fall – money you would spend shopping or saving for a wish list item, eating out, traveling, entertaining yourself, and whatever else it is that you would typically do to enjoy your life.

If You Have Children

When creating your budget, be sure to include not only your own expenses but also those of your children. School activities, clothes, trips out, and weekend activities are all things that should be budgeted. This way, you know exactly how to plan out your income each month.

Kids' activities and outings can cost a lot of money. From paying entry fees at amusement parks and zoos to buying food and drinks, it can get really pricey. So take advantage of free activities you can do with your kids. Many museums offer free days, or you can pack a nice lunch and go on a picnic. If you're looking for other free things to do with your kids, Pinterest has tons of ideas!

You also want to ensure that your emergency fund covers your children. Your goal for your emergency fund should be to have three to six months of your basic living expenses put away in the event of a true emergency, such as a job loss. It's also a good idea to include your children's basic expenses as part of your emergency account.

Finally, be sure to include a line item in your budget for saving for your child's future.

If You Have Debt

If you have debt (credit cards, student loans, auto loans, or personal loans), you should plan to pay as much as you can toward your debt each month. To do this, you'll have to lower the amounts you contribute to your different budget categories and reallocate your funds to paying off your debt as quickly as you can.

For example, if you are trying to pay off a credit card balance, your approach could be as follows:

1. Get a small emergency fund in place ($1000 can cover most basic emergencies).
2. Reduce or pause all your other savings.
3. Aggressively pay down your debt and, once that's done, fully fund your emergency account and restart saving toward your other goals.

If You Need to Catch Up on Your Retirement Savings

Again, you'd need to make adjustments to your budget categories to accommodate extra savings toward your retirement by shifting things around or cutting back in some areas altogether.

For instance, you could cut back on the "everything else" category and instead apply those funds to your retirement accounts.

A Note on Housing Costs

Keep in mind that regardless of the breakdown you choose, you want to be careful spending more than 30% of your income on just housing alone, otherwise you won't be able to put as much money toward your other goals.

There are, however, many cities in which the cost of housing is so high, that you may find that you are spending well over 30% of your income on housing costs. If you are in this situation, you can explore housing options like getting a roommate, moving to a more affordable neighborhood, moving to the suburbs further away from the main city, or downsizing to a smaller place.

■ ■ ■

With a budget in place, you'll be well on your way to paying down your debts, building your net worth, and achieving your financial goals. Think of your budget as a money management tool that makes saving and spending much easier – why wouldn't you want that?

Keep in mind, though, that there are many different ways to track and allocate your finances. In the next chapter, I'll show you a couple of options that might work for you.

BUDGETING STYLES

One of the reasons so many people shy away from budgeting is that it can seem tedious, annoying, and even difficult. As a result, they struggle with successfully creating and sticking to their budget. However, there are a variety of ways to budget – and your success with budgeting can be greatly improved by changing your budgeting style.

Who said style was just for the way you dress? Your budget can have style too!

The style you choose is entirely up to you. The most important part is picking one that works for your life and one that you (can grow to) like, even if you currently hate budgeting. In fact, you can just try one that sounds great. If it doesn't work for you, you can switch styles until you find your groove. The point is that you need to figure out a way to budget that works with your personality and personal style. Because budgeting is important, there really should be no excuse for not doing it. So in this section I'm going to outline four budgeting styles you can try.

TIP

The best type of budgeting style is the one that works best for you.

The Percentage Breakdown

This is a popular budgeting style – in fact, it's probably the most common one. You got a taste of this in the last section where I outlined some budget categories to follow. In this method, you break your income into percentages and then plan out your spending and savings accordingly. The most popular percentage breakdown is the 50–30–20 budgeting method, which is as follows:

- Your needs/essentials (shelter, food, transportation, insurance) – 50%
- Your wants/nonessentials (travel, entertainment, dining out, hobbies) – 30%
- Money for the future (retirement savings, kids' college funds), your emergency fund, debt repayment beyond the minimum required payments, and other long-term goals – 20%

Keep in mind that these percentages are not set in stone. For instance, you can choose to spend less on your needs/essentials and wants/nonessentials and put more toward savings or debt.

Some other common percentage breakdowns include:

- 80–20:

  20% of your income is allocated toward savings and debt, while the remaining 80% covers both your essential and nonessential expenses.
- 70–20–10:

  70% of your income is allocated toward your essential and nonessential expenses, 20% of your income is set aside for savings, and the remaining 10% is used to pay down debt.
- 60–30–10:

  60% of your income goes toward savings, debt payoff, and investments, 30% is budgeted for your essential expenses, and 10% is for nonessentials.
- 30–30–30–10

  30% of your income goes toward your housing costs, 30% goes toward your savings goals, 30% pays for your essential expenses including debt, and the final 10% is for nonessentials.

As you review your needs/essentials, wants/nonessentials, and your savings and debt repayment goals, you may even decide to select a 35/30/35 breakdown, a 35/35/40 breakdown, or even a 25/25/50 breakdown. Ultimately, the goal is to set percentage breakdowns that make sense for you.

Who This Budgeting Style Is Good For

If your income and expenses are fixed for the most part, and you want a clear-cut approach to splitting up your finances, this approach would work well for you. To be successful with it, you want to make sure that you look closely at your breakdown and adjust things as necessary based on your financial situation. Ultimately, the goal with your percentages should be to help you improve your financial situation, whether that is paying off debt or saving more.

The Envelope or Cash System

This works by subtracting your expenses from your income and then putting each expense amount into its own envelope. This would include things like bills you need to pay and your day-to-day spending.

You can keep the money for your big bills in virtual envelopes that you track through a spreadsheet or app and then put actual cash for your smaller expenses or day-to-day transactions in actual physical envelopes.

Once the envelope for a particular expense is depleted, you can no longer spend money in that category unless it is an emergency. If you don't spend all the money in a particular expense envelope, you can repurpose the funds toward something else like savings or debt.

Who This Budgeting Style Is Good For

If you struggle with sticking to a budget or with overspending, then this budget approach could work well for you. That's because it's harder to spend cash than it is to spend money on a debit or credit card – you actually see the dollar bills leaving your envelopes!

With this method, you are clear about what money is meant for what part of your budget. If you do choose this method, be mindful of where you keep your envelopes. Since you'll be operating partially or wholly in cash, you want to be sure you don't lose anything!

Reverse Budgeting

Reverse budgeting is a method where you focus on a single goal, such as paying off a certain amount of debt or saving a certain amount of money each month in addition to paying your bills. And then, as long as you meet your monthly goal and pay your bills without exceeding your income, you can do what you like with the money you have left over.

Who This Budgeting Style Is Good For

This approach could work for you if your finances are simple, you have fixed bills, and you're following a savings or debt repayment strategy that fits into your current income.

You'd still want to make sure you are aware of and are tracking all your bills, debt payments, and savings amounts so you can monitor your payments and track your progress toward accomplishing your goals.

Using Apps

Apps make it really simple to budget, especially if you can connect your bank accounts to them. They eliminate the manual aspect of tracking your transactions – for the most part, all you need to do is check in frequently to ensure your transactions are tracked the right way and set up alerts to keep you on top of your budget.

You can set up your budget to be reflective of any of the above budgeting methods.

Who This Budgeting Style Is Good For

Budgeting with an app basically automates your tracking, which can make things really simple. At the same time, it can detach you from closely monitoring your finances if you don't make a conscious effort to do so. You want to make sure that if you are using an app, you are checking in on your budget frequently and reviewing your category breakdowns to ensure your app is accurately matching your transactions to the right budget categories.

■ ■ ■

If you are undecided about which approach to use, test each out for a month to determine what works best for you based on which one is easiest to use and fits into your money management style. You might also choose to use a hybrid or combination of these different styles.

Ultimately, when it comes to budgeting, whatever is easiest is best. The easier or more manageable you make it, the more likely you are to do it – and that's what truly matters here. Like I mentioned earlier, budgeting is one of the foundational pieces when it comes to financial success, so in order to succeed, what matters is that you follow the budget you set.

Take Action

Work on creating a brand-new budget or adjust your existing one with these tips (see the appendix for a simple personal budget template):

- Add up all your sources of regular income.
- Next, list all of your expenses for each month. This will include your fixed costs like rent/mortgage, utilities, and insurance, as well as your variable costs like groceries, entertainment, and transportation. Don't forget to include your savings (paying yourself first) and debt repayments as expenses.
- If you aren't sure what all of your expenses are, go over the last three months of your bank and credit card statements to see what you pay for on a recurring basis.
- In addition, review the expenses you know you have coming up in the month and include those items in your budget as well.

- Add up the numbers to determine your income versus your expenses.
- If your expenses exceed your income, brainstorm where you can cut back and/or how you can earn more.
- If your income covers your expenses, challenge yourself to widen the gap between your income and your expenses. Again, brainstorm where you can cut back and/or how you can earn more.

If you haven't already settled on a budgeting style, use the following steps to determine which one could work best for you:

1. Pick a style to test out for a month.
2. Establish your budget based on the style and then set reminders to actively track your budget at least once a week.
3. As you make progress throughout the month, take note of what is working and what isn't when it comes to that particular style.
4. If you find that it doesn't work for you, test out a new style the following month, using the steps above.

DON'T IGNORE YOUR MONEY LEAKS

One important thing to keep in mind is that even though you are budgeting consistently, you might not be aware of your money leaks!

A money leak refers to small amounts of spending, or expenses you don't pay attention to or are unaware of that slowly impact your finances over time. Think of it as having tiny holes in your budget, from which money slowly leaks out when you aren't paying attention. When added up over time, these leaks can be a significant amount of money.

But how do these money leaks happen when you create and track your budget on a consistent basis? Well, you may find that you are not tracking your spending in as much detail as you should be because life happens, and you get busy. Or you already know you have certain amounts allocated to certain categories in your budget and so you tell yourself that if you don't exceed the amount for that category, your budget is fine. (I've been guilty of this!)

But could some of that money be put to better use? And are you sure you are not overpaying for certain expenses? This is where you'll find those money leaks!

Are you aware of any money leaks in your budget? Here are some costs you should pay attention to that are responsible for the biggest money leaks:

1. Food and groceries

   The cost of food continues to rise and eating out on a consistent basis can eat up a huge chunk of your budget. And so being mindful of how much you are spending on food particularly can have a significant impact on your budget.

   To plug this leak, assess your fridge and your pantry to see what you have at home and then create a food list before you go grocery shopping. When you shop, be sure to look out for your grocery store offers and sales.

   You can also consider meal planning to reduce how often you eat out or order in. Eating out comes with a higher price tag than cooking at home and those food delivery fees can add up to a big deal over time!

2. Subscriptions

   In today's world, there's a subscription for pretty much everything, from entertainment streaming services to personal care products to pet products to meal services and more. Individually, many subscriptions are reasonably priced, but when you have multiple subscriptions, the amount can add up.

   So if you are paying for subscriptions (or memberships) you hardly ever use, it's time to cancel them!

3. Brand-name products

   We all love a good brand name, but the truth is, there are several generic or store-brand alternatives that are just as good if not better than some of the brand-name items. It's worth exploring generic and store-brand alternatives to save some extra cash.

   For example, instead of the big brand names, I buy store-brand frozen vegetables. They taste the same in my opinion! So save the cash where there's no difference, and this way you can splurge on the brand names you love.

4. Credit card interest

   If you can afford to pay more than the minimum on your credit cards each month but you don't, then that's a big money leak! This is because of the accruing compounding interest on your debt. Paying more than the minimum on your credit card reduces the compounding interest you'll accrue.

5. Not comparing prices

   Don't get comfortable with your cell phone, cable, or insurance bill; shop around for better deals! I have a reminder to do this once a year. It only takes a few minutes and if I find a better deal, I let my current provider know.

   Many times, they will match the rates I find without me having to switch service providers. The savings is totally worth those few minutes of your time.

Other common money leaks include things like:

- Purchasing more than you need because of discounts or promotions. Umm, no, you don't need to spend an extra $50 to get free shipping when shipping costs $3.99!
- Recurring bank fees and charges. It's worth shopping around to find the free checking and savings accounts.

- Paying for services you can easily do yourself. Pay to get your nails done if that brings you joy but you can watch a YouTube video to hang up a painting and save yourself the handyman fee!

Plugging your money leaks requires that you stay aware of where your money is going. By doing this, you can avoid wasting money and put the money you don't spend toward the things that bring you joy or toward paying down debt, saving, or investing!

TIP

It's a good idea to do an assessment of any potential money leaks you might have every few months so you can stay on top of things.

Take Action

Use the following steps to find and plug any money leaks you might have:

1. Look for patterns or trends in your spending. Are there areas where you consistently overspend or make impulse purchases? Are there any bills or services you are paying too much for or don't need altogether?
2. Once you've identified your money leaks, what specific things can you do to cut back on those expenses? For example, are there opportunities for you to negotiate lower rates on things like certain utilities or car insurance or can you switch to more cost-effective providers?

By following these steps and taking action, you can effectively plug your money leaks.

COMMON BUDGETING CHALLENGES AND HOW TO GET OUT OF YOUR OWN WAY

Even if you are tracking your budget consistently and have plugged all your money leaks, there are still several challenges, especially mindset and behavior-related challenges, that can come up as you manage your budget and work on your financial goals.

So let's talk about some common budgeting challenges and how to tackle them if you find yourself faced with one or more of these challenges!

Being indecisive about your finances

Financial indecisiveness is totally normal, but it doesn't have to hold you back from being successful with your money. The mere thought of making money decisions can be challenging, but just diving in is the best move. The longer you put it off, the more it'll weigh on your mind. Indecision is a big hurdle when it comes to financial planning, but with a little push, you can conquer it.

First things first – schedule some dedicated time on your calendar to lay out your money goals and then create a simple budget. Don't stress about things being perfect; just start putting it together. Once you've got that in place, you can tackle any bumps that come your way, one step at a time.

Next up, automate your finances. Set your bills to pay themselves every month automatically, including your savings. It takes the pressure off decision-making because things just happen without you having to think about it too much.

And don't be afraid to seek help if you need it. Talking to a financial pro like a certified financial planner (CFP) or a financial therapist can really ease that indecisive feeling. They can help you figure out your goals and how to make the best choices for your money, now and in the future.

Constantly impulse shopping

One of the toughest parts about sticking to a budget is giving in to those spur-of-the-moment shopping urges. Let's face it, we've all been there. (My hand is raised!) In fact, the average American drops about $150 a month on impulse buys.[1]

To tackle this challenge, you've got to get real about what's triggering your shopping sprees. Often, there's something deeper going on than just wanting stuff. Figuring out what's really bothering you instead of hitting the mall when you're feeling down can help drown out those impulsive urges.

Next time you feel that itch to splurge, pause and write down how you're feeling and what's been going on. You might realize that shopping is just a Band-Aid for a bigger issue, and the first step to breaking free is getting support.

It's also smart to cut back on how often you're hitting the stores or scrolling through online shops. Temptation is everywhere, so sometimes it's best to limit your exposure. Designate a chunk of cash specifically for planned shopping trips. This way, you can treat yourself without blowing your budget.

Being afraid of your debt

You know the saying "Ignorance is bliss"? Well, when it comes to your finances, that couldn't be further from the truth. Ignoring your debt won't make it disappear; in fact, it can cause it to snowball and it can even mess up your credit score.

While it's natural to feel apprehensive about debt, it's important not to let fear paralyze you. Debt can be managed effectively with a clear plan. By taking proactive steps and staying focused, you can overcome debt and work toward a healthier financial future for yourself. We'll dive into tackling debt in the next chapter.

---

[1] https://www.statista.com/statistics/1330467/per-month-spending-on-impulse-purchases-usa

Not budgeting to save money

Just because you're paying your bills on time doesn't necessarily mean you've got your budgeting game on point. If you're not setting aside some cash for savings, you're missing out on prepping for your future.

When it comes to budgeting, one of the smartest moves you can make is paying yourself first, no matter how small the amount. Building savings into your budget is key because it helps you form solid money habits.

I remember making $1 deposits into my savings account early on in my financial journey. Saving what I could, no matter how small the amount was, helped me stay consistent, and over time, as I earned more money, saving became second nature because I'd already established the habit.

To kick-start your savings game, allocate a percentage of your paycheck or a fixed amount to go straight into your savings account. You can even set up automatic transfers so you don't even have to think about it.

Not budgeting consistently

Sticking to your budget regularly sets you up for success. Being consistent helps you avoid excessive splurging and keeps your finances in check.

Make it a habit to give your budget a once-over regularly. I do a quick five-minute check at the end of each day, but you can create a cadence that works for you, whether that's every day, every other day, or once a week.

If your bills go up or your income changes, you'll want to make sure your budget reflects that. Set a reminder on your calendar to review your finances on the regular – it'll help you stay on top of things and keep your budget on track.

REWARDING YOURSELF

The truth is, you work so hard for your money! So it's only fair that you get to reward yourself every now and then, right? Well, yes! You definitely deserve to treat yourself and have fun – what girl doesn't love to look good, take nice trips, and enjoy life?! #softlifeliving.

However, when it comes to rewards and spending money, you want to make sure you are doing it the right way by spending smartly and not derailing your financial goals. So how do you reward yourself and still stay on top of those goals you set?

You need to plan accordingly, and here's how.

Designate Some Fun Money in Your Budget

All work and no play is never any fun, especially if you're working hard to earn your money. That being said, working hard and playing excessively can be detrimental when it comes to your finances. Feeling like you deserve something and then overspending is the biggest culprit when it comes to derailed financial goals.

You can avoid this by building your rewards (your fun money) into your budget each month. That is, once all your essentials have been met! This way, you don't feel like your budget is a punishment. Because you've given yourself wiggle room, you'll feel like your budget allows you to treat yourself and you won't feel deprived.

If you want to purchase something that costs more than your monthly fun money allocation, plan to save part of your fun money over a few months. The result? Guilt-free spending, and your financial goals will remain intact.

If you have debt, a great approach is to reward yourself in a small way each time you pay off a chunk of money.

Reward Yourself with the Things That Matter to You

It's important to ensure that as you reward yourself, you are spending your money on things and experiences that you really want and truly value. Why? Because the more in-tune you are with spending money on the things you value, the less likely you are to feel discontentment, which can lead to overspending.

For example, if you value spending time with loved ones, then your fun money can go toward experiences with them, like dinners out, going to the movies, or spending a day at an amusement park. If this is something you value, remember that you don't need to spend money to have a good time. Maybe instead of going out for dinner, you have a special dinner at home. Or, if you want to watch a movie together, cue the Netflix and homemade popcorn! You're very likely to find yourself feeling happy, grateful, and content when you choose to treat yourself with things and experiences you really value.

On the other hand, if you spend your fun money on things you don't really care about, you might find yourself spending more and more to find that next great thing. You'll be left feeling unsatisfied and feel the need to spend even more. So when it comes to your fun money, be flexible with what you spend it on, but figure out what truly satisfies you and make that your priority.

Reward Yourself for Free

As I mentioned, rewards don't always have to be about spending money. You can reward yourself for free in so many ways! Examples include finding free entertainment (free museum days and events in your city), having potluck nights in with your friends and family, or using loyalty or rewards points you have accumulated instead of spending cash.

Taking time out for some quality "me-time" is a fantastic way to treat yourself, and it's something I make sure to do regularly. In our fast-paced world, it's crucial to prioritize self-care so you can recharge every now and then.

Whether it's pampering yourself with an at-home spa day using items you already have, diving into a good book, going for a leisurely walk or hike, or simply taking a day to unwind, there are plenty of ways to do it. Consider unplugging from the digital world for a bit too; it can really help reduce stress. You'll be amazed at how much better you feel afterward!

If You Don't Need to Spend It, Save It

Ever find yourself not wanting or needing to reward yourself all the time? Take that money you have in your budget and repurpose it toward your financial goals! Put it in your savings or investment account, or be charitable. Just because you've put aside money doesn't mean you need to spend it (all) if you don't really have to. If you're satisfied with what you've done this month and you have money left over, don't force yourself to spend it!

Don't Get Caught Up in Comparison; Be Content with What You Have

A lot of the time, people end up spending money they don't have on things they don't really want – usually because someone else has it or expects you to have it. My philosophy on this is don't feel like you need to spend money to impress anyone. You've probably heard the saying that comparison is the thief of joy, and it really is. Don't spend money you don't need to spend to impress anyone; otherwise, you'll find yourself competing way past what your budget allows. Be happy with what you have and what you like, and forget about what other people think!

If you are rewarding yourself, do it because you really want to, and you are going to be happy about what you spend your money on – for you.

Take Action

Use the following steps to create a plan to reward yourself without breaking your budget:

1. Open a separate account where you can put money aside to reward yourself guilt-free.
2. Go over your budget and see if there's any room to include small amounts that you can transfer into the designated account you have established.
3. Make a wish list of what you'd like to do or buy and determine how much it will cost. This will give you a good idea of how long it will take you to save for it.

4. It's important to keep in mind that you don't want rewarding yourself to take you off your path to achieving your financial goals, so keep it realistic and within reason.

MEET ESTHER BANGURA

Esther is a certified financial planner in the UK and the host of the podcast *Boss of My Money*. She knows firsthand the challenges of managing finances and is dedicated to using her experience to help other women overcome their financial struggles and achieve their financial goals.

Esther shares how she leveraged budgeting to transform her finances and pay off over $23,000 of debt in just 22 months despite a 55% reduction of her household income.

Can you walk us through the circumstances that led to the 55% reduction of your household income?

> A few years ago, my husband and I decided that it was time for a career change. While the decision to change careers seemed exciting, I had no idea how much sacrifice and change I would have to make. This career change would mean both of us working part-time, and me losing 55% of my salary, with no savings set aside to support our transition.
>
> Prior to working part-time to support my career change, I earned about $65,000 per year. With the comfort of our two incomes, my husband and I were blindly paying bills, using credit cards, and repeating the paycheck-to-paycheck cycle.

What motivated you to start budgeting despite facing such a challenging financial situation?

> After losing 55% of my income and realizing I would be over $1000 short every month, I knew I had to face the music and get a handle on my finances.

Each month, I would have to prioritize my expenses and decide which provider would receive payment that month.

Around this time, I enrolled in the Clever Girl Finance Accountability Program. This was where I first learned about budgeting and how it can help me plan my money. My motivation to start budgeting, even though I was over $1000 short each month, stemmed from the idea of using budgeting as a planning tool and holding myself accountable to that plan. Additionally, being a part of a community not only provided me with a safe space to share my challenges and plans for improving my situation, but it also assisted me in overcoming the shame and guilt associated with the financial mistakes I had made in the past.

Could you describe the budgeting strategies you implemented to adapt to your new financial reality?

Initially, I used budgeting apps and spreadsheets, but I felt overwhelmed. I needed a simple budgeting method that would work for where I was with my finances, so I created one myself. I had great success with an A4 notebook, pen, paper, and calculator. Manually recording each expense and adding the numbers up in my calculator helped me connect more with my finances. As a result, I felt more in control and confident in my ability to develop and stick to a solid plan.

I learned about zero-based budgeting through the accountability program and over time, as I became more comfortable with my numbers and knew exactly how much my bills were, I was able to switch to using budgeting spreadsheets. This made budgeting much easier because I had a template for each month and any changes would be calculated automatically.

Can you share some of the key adjustments or sacrifices you had to make in your spending habits to align with your budget?

> The first adjustment was to my food budget and shopping frequency. I set aside $100 each week and shopped weekly rather than monthly. I stopped shopping at Costco monthly and only went for necessary bulk items. Eliminating food waste saved me a lot of money on my grocery bill and overall budget.
>
> The second adjustment was to decline invitations to birthday, wedding, and graduation parties from friends and family members. This was the most difficult thing I ever did. First, I had to tell my close friends and family that I was in debt and living paycheck to paycheck. As difficult as it was to tell them, combined with the fear of being judged, they felt relieved as they too shared their own financial struggles with me. It was not that I turned down every single event invitation, though. During this period, I was able to build stronger friendships and connect more with my family by being creative about celebrating with them. For example, hosting potlucks.
>
> The third change was to avoid using credit altogether. I stopped using my credit card and instead relied on my debit card to pay bills and I only used cash for groceries. I realized that the only way my debt would start declining was if I stopped adding to it. At the time, I was $23,000 in debt and was able to pay it off in 22 months by making these three key changes.

How did you prioritize your expenses during this period?

> To align with my income and budgeting style, I leveraged a percentage-based method to pay myself first. With this approach, I contributed 10%, invested 5%,

and saved 5%. The rest I allocated to priority bills such as rent, utilities, travel, and insurance; fixed recurring nonessential bills such as monthly subscriptions, food, and anything I could cancel with 30 days' notice; and variable bills such as quarterly and annual bills.

I also set aside a fun allowance (and still do). This was essentially my predetermined monthly pocket money. I could use it for salon visits, eating out, and shopping. I then used the debt snowball method to prioritize my debt repayments. I paid the minimum on all of them and added an extra $130 each month until it was completely paid off.

Did you encounter any unexpected challenges or setbacks while implementing your budgeting plan, and if so, how did you overcome them?

Experiencing setbacks while attempting to create and stick to a budget can be disheartening. With such a low income, it took me a while to accumulate my first emergency fund of $1300.

On two occasions, my car was hit by an unknown driver while parked. This meant that I had to pay the deductible on two insurance claims to get the car fixed. Although I was annoyed this occurred, I learned that you don't realize how important it is to have savings until you need it and have it available!

Looking back, what do you believe were the most crucial factors that contributed to your success in transforming your finances despite the significant loss of income?

Increasing my financial literacy had a significant impact on my transformation. Learning about my financial personality, learning how to budget, having access to budgeting tools, and being part of a supportive community were all important factors.

If you don't know where you are going, you'll end up someplace else.

–Yogi Berra

#CLEVERGIRLSKNOW

BUDGETING ON AN INCONSISTENT INCOME

If you work infrequently, part-time, or you're a freelancer, you probably have a somewhat inconsistent income each month, making budgeting that much more difficult. If this is you, just know that it is possible to budget successfully, even if you're not sure exactly how much you'll make each month.

When it comes to budgeting on an inconsistent income, the best way to approach it is with flexibility. This will allow you to be successful at managing your money, and I'm going to show one strategy you can use to make budgeting a success in your life:

1. **Create a baseline budget.** You can also call this your bare minimum budget. This is basically a list of all your necessities and expenses that you absolutely need to pay to get by each month. The total amount of these expenses is the minimum amount of money you'd need to earn.

   This would include things like your rent or mortgage, your core utilities, food, and transportation. This does not include going out to eat, shopping, or entertainment – remember, it's the bare minimum amount of money that you need to get by.

   Since your income is inconsistent, you can take the average of your last three to six months of pay to come up with an income number to plan your budget around.
2. **Prioritize your expenses.** Once you create your baseline budget, the next step is to prioritize your expenses in order of importance. This means determining which bills need to be paid first and which ones can wait for now.

   For instance, housing, food, utilities, and transportation could be items 1–4 on your list. Having this priority in place ensures that you are properly allocating your money to your top budget items each time you get paid. So even if your paycheck does not cover everything in your budget, you have the important things paid for.

3. **Plan for future months when you earn more.** If you happen to earn more money in a certain month, pay for your most important expenses first and then plan to put aside some money in an emergency fund. This will cover future months when your income is lower. This way, you can cover your expenses during those months without going into debt. Make it a point to contribute to your emergency account before you spend on any non-essentials.
4. **Increase your income.** If you're finding that it's difficult to manage your upswings and downswings in your income, find other ways to increase the amount of money you make. Consider getting rid of things you don't need or getting a part-time job to help balance out the swings. This way, aside from just paying your bills, you can start to save and invest too.

Take Action

Work on creating a baseline budget:

1. List the necessities and expenses you need to get by each month. Consider your rent/mortgage, food, utilities, and transportation costs. This amount is the minimum you'll need to earn to cover your expenses. Align these expenses to the average of your income over the last three to six months.
2. Plan to save a small percentage of your earnings if you can, especially in high-earning months, toward future months where you might not earn enough. Over time, this amount should cover your basic expenses for a few months.
3. Next, start thinking of ways you can increase your income. Ultimately, your goal should be to earn more and establish more consistency with your earnings.

BUDGETING ON A LOW INCOME

Similarly to budgeting on an inconsistent income, managing your finances when you have a low income can be challenging and stressful. The key difference, however, between an inconsistent income and a low income is that with a low income, you are consistently earning a small amount of money, while with an inconsistent income, your earnings fluctuate over periods of time and are not necessarily low.

So many people assume that it's impossible to budget or plan when your income is consistently low, but that is not true. You can lay out your financial goals and create a budget to help you succeed with your finances, even on a low income.

By taking these actions now, you are being intentional about managing your finances as best as possible on your current income. You are also laying the groundwork to do well with your money when your income increases because based on your current actions, you would have established your habits and built the consistency around budgeting.

Even if you are having to leverage debt right now, until your income increases, you can still budget to ensure you are leveraging only the amount you need to, until you can pay it off.

As you work on increasing your income, here are some key tips to help you budget on a low income in the meantime:

1. **Track your expenses and cut unnecessary costs.** You absolutely need to be aware of where every dollar you earn goes because on a low income, every single dollar has a job to do for you. So start a spending journal for the next 30 days to see where your money is really going each month. This means tracking everything (bills, groceries, eating out, miscellaneous spending, etc.).

   As you do this, take a good look at your spending habits. Is there anything you can cut back on temporarily or even permanently? For instance, do you have subscriptions you don't use or need? Can you cook at home instead of eating out as often? Do you need to adjust your living expenses by moving to a cheaper place or getting a roommate?

2. **Prioritize your needs first.** When money is tight, focusing on your core essentials first is key. This means making sure your money goes to costs like housing, food, necessary utilities, and transportation, before any nonessential spending. It's all about ensuring your basic needs are met first.
3. **Explore assistance programs.** Depending on where you live, you might have access to community resources or government programs that help low-income earners minimize their financial strain. Many of these programs help with housing, utilities, food, and healthcare. There is no shame whatsoever in seeking this assistance if you need it. After all, you are reading this book because you want to improve your finances, and this assistance can help keep you afloat while you work on pursuing your financial goals and improving your financial situation.

   Some assistance programs for low-income earners include:

   - **Supplemental Nutrition Assistance Program (SNAP)** provides eligible individuals and families with funds to purchase nutritious food items. Website: https://www.fns.usda.gov/snap/supplemental-nutrition-assistance-program
   - **Low-Income Home Energy Assistance Program (LIHEAP)** assists eligible households with their heating and cooling costs, particularly during extreme weather conditions. Website: https://www.acf.hhs.gov/ocs/programs/liheap
   - **Rental assistance** is offered through several government programs to help individuals and families find

affordable rental housing. Website to review housing programs: https://www.usa.gov/rental-housing-programs

You can also look up assistance programs in your local community through online searches. Many local organizations and charities provide assistance to individuals and families facing financial hardship.

Take Action

1. Get a notebook that's easy to carry around or use the notes app on your phone to track your spending over the next 30 days so you are aware exactly where your money is going.
2. Write out your essential expenses and determine what nonessential expenses you can cut back on temporarily or permanently.
3. Explore assistance programs if you need to.

BUDGETING AS A COUPLE

If you've taken the leap to settle down with a significant other, congratulations! This is a great time to figure out your finances together. Inevitably, money will become a factor in your relationship as you plan out your living expenses and long-term goals, so you might as well get started as soon as possible.

While being in a relationship can be considerably cheaper than living independently, managing your finances as a couple can sometimes be stressful and can cause many disagreements. For example, if one person earns significantly more than the other, splitting your bills 50/50 might leave one side stressed and even resentful. Or perhaps one of you is a shopper and the other is a saver – many arguments about overspending may be in your future.

The good news is that it's usually a lack of communication that ends up being the root cause of why couples struggle to budget successfully. If you can manage to keep lines of communication open and get your budget settled from the start, your finances don't need to become a source of stress or arguments in your life together.

How do you do it? Here are a few of my best tips:

1. **Plan a monthly money conversation.** Having a conversation with your significant other about money allows you to lay out your money plans and create a budget you can both agree on. Usually, it's most helpful if you do this in advance of each month; for example, in July you would plan August's budget. These conversations give you the opportunity to talk about the bills and expenses you know are coming up. This way, there are no surprises, your dollars are allocated in advance, and you don't have to stress about not knowing what your partner is spending.

   In these conversations, it's important to be transparent with each other and share what's really going on. I've talked to a lot of women who are hiding debt from their significant others, afraid of what could happen if they shared it with them. However, lying and hiding your problems doesn't make them go away. The longer you keep secrets, the worse it will be when your partner eventually finds out.

   My advice is to bring it to the table, along with a plan on how you intend to deal with the situation. Yes, they might be upset, but they might also have something they need to get off their chest and share with you as well. Keeping the lines of communication open means you'll both be on the same page and be able to attack issues together. Taking the first step to being transparent with your finances can greatly improve your relationship and your financial future.

2. **Talk about your long-term goals.** Your money conversations shouldn't be just about your monthly budget. Take some time out to talk about your dreams and goals and how you plan to approach them. Want to start a business? Travel more? Save more money toward retirement? These are conversations you should be having often that will help you plan together as a team. A good idea is to create specific categories within your budget that you both agree on. Don't forget to include saving for your long-term goals.
3. **Listen and communicate.** Communication is the foundation of success in any relationship and in budgeting together as a couple. There will be times where you don't always agree on your money choices, but the key to getting past disagreements is to listen, communicate your point of view, and come to a mutual agreement. Remember, you are a team, not rivals.
4. **Stick to the plan you both agree on.** Once your budget is set, don't deviate from it without first having a conversation about it. Not only will this avoid conflict, but it will help you maintain trust with your significant other around your finances. The last thing you want is to get into a big fight or feel disappointed because one of you didn't honor the agreement you both made.

   If you struggle with following a budget, let your partner know. You can work together to improve your budgeting skills and come up with solutions together. Differences in style don't need to become arguments or resentment.
5. **Do what works best for you as a couple.** When it comes to how you manage your finances and where you keep your money, do what works best for you. Chances are you and your partner will have different money management styles. When it comes to budgeting and managing money, that could mean you'll need to compromise

on what you're used to doing to accommodate your partner by finding a hybrid solution you can both work with.

When it comes to the types of accounts you hold, you might decide to have separate accounts, joint accounts, or a combination of the two. Remember that it's not worth it to compare yourself with others, so don't worry too much about what other couples are doing with their money. What works for one couple may not necessarily work for you – the last thing you want is to have issues in your relationship based on what other people are doing in theirs.

6. **Keep yourself in mind.** Sharing finances with a partner can be intimidating. Being practical in how you manage your money might not be the most romantic idea, but it might save you a lot of stress in the future. As you plan your finances with your partner, be sure you both keep yourselves in mind as well.

   In the event that things don't go as planned (and unfortunately, this happens), have a plan in place for what you'll do with your finances – and don't neglect your own financial needs while in your relationship. Keep contributing to your retirement savings and establishing your own assets and income. If you do end up separating, you'll have something to bounce back on.

Take Action

If talking about money is a challenge in your relationship, schedule some time with your significant other to start having those money conversations. Here are a few suggestions:

1. Put a time on the calendar in advance of each month for a conversation about your budget and overall finances in a relaxed setting.

2. If necessary, plan what you'd like to discuss ahead of time. You can also plan to split up the conversation into multiple sessions so it doesn't become overwhelming. This can be particularly helpful when you're just starting out.
3. Keep in mind that conversations about money are not battles. Managing your finances together is about both of you aligning your finances to your long-term goals as a team. Work together and keep communication as open as possible.

Cash is queen.

#CLEVERGIRLSKNOW

THE SAVE YOURSELF FUND: YOUR EMERGENCY SAVINGS

Your car breaks down, your water heater breaks, you lose your job and can't find a new one, you have a medical emergency. Yup, life happens! And when it does, it comes with all kinds of financial surprises. This is where your emergency savings comes in.

Although I have mentioned having an emergency fund a few times now, I think it's important enough to warrant its own section. As the name indicates, your emergency savings is to help you weather unplanned life circumstances or emergencies. Having a stash of cash to fall back on when "life happens" means you won't have to rely on credit or rack up debt in order to resolve your situation. It helps you stay ready.

Although your emergency fund isn't super-fun to save up for, not having one can cause financial stress. In many cases where emergency savings have not been established, people end up taking on additional debt, significantly setting them back on any progress they might have made with their financial goals. So while it's not exactly romantic or exciting to save up an emergency fund, it can offer peace of mind and, of course, support you in times of need.

Just like with the word *budget*, if you don't like the word *emergency*, call it something you like, something that will motivate you to get it funded.

How Much Do I Need in Emergency Savings?

Ideally, your goal should be to have at least three to six months of your essential living expenses in emergency savings. This includes living expenses related to your housing, transportation, and food needs. It should cover your core essentials, not your wants or splurges, so it doesn't have to be extravagant.

If you are single, the more you have saved, the better, so setting a goal of at least six months would be wise. If you are married or in a relationship where you have a second income to fall back on, you can start with three months of savings as a goal and raise it to six later on.

If you have children (or other dependents), pets, or you own a home, make sure you add in an additional buffer to cover their essentials as well.

The more you have saved up for the unexpected, the better. Ideally, having 12 months of savings in place would be amazing, especially in advance of a bad economy or recession where job losses are more likely.

Debt and Emergency Savings

If you are, however, paying off high-interest debt, I recommend you start with an initial goal of getting your emergency savings to $1000. This amount can be saved fairly quickly and will cover most basic unplanned situations.

Once you've gotten your emergency savings to $1000, your next area of focus should be on paying down that debt as quickly as you can (we'll discuss debt in detail in the next few chapters) and then, once it's gone, shift your focus back to fully funding your emergency savings.

Focusing on paying off your debt first will potentially save you thousands of dollars in high-interest payments, so that should be your priority. For instance, it makes more financial sense to pay off debt with a 15% interest rate than to keep money in a savings account earning you only 1% interest, because over the long term you are actually losing a ton of money from the payments you are making, despite having money in savings.

How to Fund Your Emergency Savings

Saving three to six months of your income for the unexpected sounds like a lot, but don't panic! It's totally possible to have that much money put away if you save for it over time. If an unexpected situation does come up, you can use that money and then work on replenishing it once the emergency is resolved.

The best way to save for and meet your emergency savings goal is to include a category for it in your monthly budget. You can take it a step further by scheduling automated transfers to an account you have set up strictly for your emergency savings.

Where to Keep Your Emergency Savings

Your emergency fund should be easily accessible and liquid so you can get to it when you need it without having to wait and without having to worry about how financial markets are performing. Therefore, it shouldn't be tied up in investments like the stock market or in real estate. An interest-bearing savings account or a certificate of deposit are good places to keep this money.

You also want to make sure that you are keeping your emergency savings separate from your other financial goals. Blending your savings goals together can get confusing, and in the event you have to use your savings, taking the money out of a comingled account can make you feel like you are setting yourself back with your other goals as well.

I've talked to countless women who are upset or feel depressed when they have to use their emergency savings to cover an unplanned situation. However, setting it aside and keeping it separate from your other financial goals and understanding the true purpose of your emergency savings can help avoid these feelings when you have to use it.

Having an emergency fund is essential and should be part of everyone's overall financial plan. You don't want to ruin all your hard work of paying down debt and building wealth by not being prepared to handle an unplanned or unexpected life event.

Take Action

Do you already have an emergency savings account? Have one but haven't funded it yet? It's time to get on it. Use the tips here to determine how much you need to set aside:

1. If you haven't already, take some time out to determine what your essential living expenses are each month, so you know exactly how much you'll need to set aside.
2. Set an immediate goal to get your emergency savings to $1000.
3. Your next goal should be to get your savings to a full month of your basic living expenses, and then to three months and then six months. However, if you have high-interest debt, once you get your savings to $1000, you should first focus on paying down that debt as quickly as you can. Then work on fully funding your emergency savings.
4. A good idea is to set up your emergency savings at a bank separate from where you do your day-to-day banking so you are not tempted to make transfers for nonemergencies. Also, you may want to avoid getting checks or a debit card to forestall any unnecessary temptation.

SINKING FUNDS TO STAY ON TRACK

Now let's talk about sinking funds. A sinking fund is easily accessible money that you save each month toward a one-time or irregular predetermined expense that you know is going to happen. For example, say you plan to host a birthday dinner three months from now with your best friends. How will you pay for it? You don't want to tap into your emergency fund for a nonemergency and you already know paying for it by credit card isn't the best move. That's where sinking funds come to the rescue!

In this instance, you'll set up a "birthday dinner sinking fund" and save money toward it each month. By the time your event arrives, you're not worried about paying for everything at the last minute because you'll be well prepared.

Sinking funds are not just for parties and events, though! Other examples could be preventative dental work, upcoming car maintenance, home repairs, and any other expense that's outside of your usual monthly budget. The amount you save in your sinking funds will depend on the cost of the expected expense.

Without sinking fund accounts in place, you might find yourself tapping into alternative sources like your emergency fund, savings, or even resorting to your credit card. Having a sinking fund isn't just about planning for big buys; it's your ticket to staying on top of your savings game, keeping debt at bay, and giving yourself the freedom to spend without the financial strain.

Sinking Funds Versus Emergency Savings

Remember, a sinking fund is different from emergency savings. Your emergency savings are reserved for just that – emergencies related to unexpected expenses. You have no idea when they will present themselves, and you may have no control over the amount of money they demand from you. With sinking funds, on the other hand, you can anticipate the upcoming expense and plan toward it. There's no element of surprise and no changes to your other savings buckets.

What Is the Right Number of Sinking Funds?

The number of sinking funds you need is going to depend on the number of predetermined expenses you have upcoming, the timeframe, and your income. You may be able to save for several small upcoming expenses at once. Or you can prioritize your different sinking funds by timeframe and save for them, one after the other.

Building Your Sinking Funds Into Your Budget

Building your sinking funds into your budget should not be too hard to do. The beauty of these expenses is that you'll often know well in advance what they are and can comfortably budget for them or find alternatives.

You can look at your goal amount for your sinking fund and then break it down monthly, biweekly, or weekly depending on how often you get paid, and then save a certain amount toward your goal each time.

Categories will be different for most people; however, there are a few staple items you may always want to include to avoid any surprises later down the road. These include car repairs, small home repairs, and smaller medical expenses such as prescriptions and copays.

MY STORY: HOW I SAVED OVER $100,000 IN THREE YEARS

In the early part of my career, I doubled down with my saving and budgeting to amass over $100,000 in savings. I'm sharing this personal money story with you to show you exactly what you can accomplish when you focus on achieving a goal. Here, I'll tell you exactly what I did to get there, in a step-by-step breakdown.

I'll be honest and say that reaching this milestone of having $100,000 in savings was not a walk in the park. It was often frustrating and stressful, but I was able to do it – and if I could do it, so can you. My hope is that my story will inspire and motivate you to think bigger when it comes to your finances. When you are able to buckle down and focus on hitting a major milestone, the door will open for so much more.

When I first graduated from college, I got a job with a starting salary of $54,000, which was really closer to $40,000 after taxes. Three and a half years later, I had saved over $100,000. Here's how I did it:

1. **I contributed to my retirement savings via a 401(k) that was offered by my employer.** To be honest, when I first started working I had no clue what a 401(k) was or why I needed one. All I knew was that I was being offered free money from my employer. I was all over it!

   At the time, my employer matched 100% of the first 6% that I contributed to my retirement savings in the form of free money, and while I didn't max out my allowable contributions back then, I contributed close to 15% of my salary. As a result, over the first three and a half years, I was able to save about $40,000 in my retirement account, including growth from stock market performance over this period.

TIP

Contribute to a retirement plan as soon as you can and max out your allowable contributions, if possible. Can't afford to max out right away? Increase your contributions by 1% every quarter until you can. If your employer offers a match, take it! (I'll discuss more on investing in Chapter 5.)

2. **I kept my expenses low.** After my 401(k), health insurance, and tax deductions, my main monthly expenses were my car (starting at about $150), insurance (approximately $80), and my mortgage (about $900). In order to save, I focused on keeping my expenses as low as possible.

   I lived at home for six months after graduating from college before moving into my first place, which helped me really kickstart my savings. Because I was able to save on living expenses, most of my pay for those six months went toward my savings accounts. Groceries were never a big bill – ramen noodles were my friend!

Instead of going out, my friends and I usually hung out at each other's houses. I traveled a lot for work, so a lot of my lunches during the week were reimbursed. I also lived very close to work, so I didn't buy gas often. My water, Internet, and cell phone bills came in around $170 combined each month.

TIP

Getting your expenses down should be your first area of attack in your budget. Try living close to work if possible, cook at home, pack lunches, work out at home or outdoors, carpool, cut out alcohol, and use coupons and rebates when you shop – basically, get creative with ways to bring your expenses down.

---

3. **I focused on saving 40–50% of each paycheck and anything extra.** After my 401(k), and other deductions and taxes, I earned somewhere around $1350–$1400 per paycheck in the first year. I tried to save at least $500 to $700 of each one, as well as all of my yearly bonus, which was somewhere around $1500. Not much, but still something. I also saved a bulk of whatever tax return I got each year. One trick I used was that when I got a raise or promotion, I continued to live on my old budget, saving the full amount of the raise. By the end of the third year, my salary was about $74,000 before taxes.

   As a result, I saved a ton of cash very quickly – I averaged about $18,000 each year in cash savings, so after three years, I had well over $50,000 saved in cash from my full-time job.

TIP

It's not just about keeping expenses low. It's also about making a plan to save what you have left over. I made this easy for myself by having this money automatically sent to my savings account as soon as I got paid.

---

4. **I started a side hustle.** In my second year of saving, I became very interested in taking photographs. I ended up building a very successful part-time lifestyle and wedding photography business after taking a bit of money from savings to invest in an entry-level professional camera.

   I studied my craft, did a lot of free photography to start, and then raised my prices as I got better. Within a few months, I found this business growing quickly and becoming very profitable. As time went by, I began to network and make friends with as many experienced photographers as I could, who also began to refer business to me. I loved photography, and it earned me a great side income.

   The first year of my business, I earned around $10,000. The second year, I earned around $30,000. In subsequent years I earned more. I worked hard, but it was worth it. Around this time, I also started learning about investing outside of retirement funds. I used some of the money I earned from my side hustle to do that. This pushed my savings well over the $100,000 mark.

TIP

A side hustle, if set up and managed the right way, can be a huge boost to your income. If you have a hobby, consider turning it into something that can make you money on the side.

---

5. **I spent on credit but I was smart about it.** Even though I was seriously focused on saving over these three years, I still had a credit card. But the majority of this spending was using a charge card. Unlike with a credit card, with a charge card you are required to pay your balance in full each month, so although I did spend on credit, I never carried a balance. This worked out great for me because I didn't really have a choice when it came to paying the bill. I always tried to spend intelligently because I knew there was no safety net.

   I'll be honest, I wasn't always perfect with it. I got a few reality checks when I overdid it a few times, but using a charge card always reined me in and helped me plan ahead.

TIP

If you are able to qualify for one, consider getting a charge card instead of a credit card. It will help you build credit and acts just like a credit card, but doesn't allow you to carry a balance, so you can't overspend without serious consequences.

That, in a high-level summary, is how I was able to save over $100,000 in about three years.

With all of these tactics, you'll be able to amass a great amount of savings in a short time. You might have other responsibilities, a lower income, or fewer opportunities to save money. In that case, you may not be able to save $100,000 right now, but know that these strategies can be used to save any amount of money over any period of time. If you take just one of them, you can boost your savings.

Building significant savings starts with adjusting your mindset, taking a full assessment of where you currently stand, creating a strategy around your situation, keeping your expenses low, automating as much as you can, and staying focused – all of which this book is here to help you do. Over time, and with discipline and dedication, you will see results. I promise.

CHAPTER 4

Debt and Loans

Debt is normal.
Be weird.

– Dave Ramsey

#CLEVERGIRLSKNOW

LET'S TALK ABOUT DEBT. . .BECAUSE IT SUCKS

The basics: As much as we all hate debt, most of us have to admit that we've had debt at one point in time. For most people, credit cards, student loans, car notes, and personal loans are usually the big debt portfolio items.

And the truth is, debt sucks! Especially when it's tied to things that are essentially "gone with the wind" – those shopping trips years ago that you're still paying for now, all those dinner dates with your girlfriends that somehow added up to this annoying credit card debt that you are still dealing with. . .ugh.

Don't worry, you're not alone. I've been there and done that too, and I can vividly remember getting my first credit card. Why? Because it got me into a ton of trouble!

I was about 18 or 19 at the time, away from home with a part-time job on campus. While my mother supported me by paying my tuition and rent, my responsibilities were paying my phone bill, buying my own groceries, and taking care of my other personal needs. Imagine what I could afford on around $120 a week!

So after I paid my phone bill each month (about $30 way back when data was something you only heard about in James Bond movies) and bought enough Coca-Cola and ramen to survive (about $40), I managed the rest of my money accordingly and I was actually fine. Until I wasn't.

At the time, every major event or job fair always seemed to have an agent of financial destruction from the credit company with a booth decorated with balloons, offering free T-shirts and pens alongside their offers of "free money." I remember being coaxed over to one such booth where a woman told me I could get up to $2500 if I just filled out this one form. I immediately called home to tell my mother about the "practically free" money I was being offered at school. Her response? "What could you possibly need in your life that you need to buy on credit?"

Well, the next fair came around with another booth and another agent and again I was lured over by the freebies and supposedly free money. I explained to them that my mother didn't think it was a good idea and they proceeded to inform me that my mother never had to know about it. "We can send your statement directly to your on-campus address" were the exact words I heard. And with that, I immediately signed up and was approved for $2000. (Thanks to the Credit Card Accountability Responsibility and Disclosure Act of 2009, the law now prohibits the advertising, marketing, or merchandising of credit cards to students on college campuses.[1] That said, this type of targeted marketing has shifted to social media platforms.)

I cannot for the life of me tell you what I spent that $2000 on, but I can tell you I maxed out that card very quickly. I mean, I was balling out of control. When I received my first statement a few weeks later, I was perplexed.

24.99% interest? What?!

I had sleepless nights for a week thinking about my newly acquired debt and the fact that I didn't have a clue how I would pay it off – that $120 paycheck just wasn't going to cut it.

To make a long story short, I ended up spending months paying off my balance, including the hideous 24.99% interest I accumulated – way more than anything I purchased was worth!

Moral of this story: debt sucks.

The Buy Now, Pay Later Trend

These days, it seems like everywhere you look on social media, there's some kind of credit card marketing popping up. And if that isn't enough, Buy Now, Pay Later (BNPL) is the latest craze taking over.

[1]https://www.ftc.gov/sites/default/files/documents/statutes/credit-card-accountability-responsibility-and-disclosure-act-2009-credit-card-act/credit-card-pub-l-111-24_0.pdf

Imagine a way to shop where you can buy what you want now and pay for it later in smaller chunks – that's BNPL in a nutshell, kind of like a modern-day layaway plan but without the waiting. It has become extremely popular, especially for online shopping and buying things like clothes and electronics, because it gives you the flexibility to spend without needing all the money upfront. Plus, it's usually easy to sign up for, often with no credit check required.

Here's the deal, though. With a layaway plan, you don't get your hands on the goods until you've paid in full. But with BNPL, you can start enjoying your purchase right away and pay it off later in weekly, biweekly, or monthly installments, depending on your plan. Pretty cool, right? But hold up, there's a catch.

If you stick to the payment schedule, you're golden. But miss a payment or pay late, and you're looking at some hefty penalties and fees – sometimes up to 25% of what you owe! And here's the kicker: any payments over 30 days late can impact your credit score negatively since BNPL companies report to the credit bureaus.

Additionally, BNPL makes impulse buying way too easy. You don't have to stop and check your bank balance or think about upcoming bills. You just click, buy, and worry about paying later. It's a recipe for overspending and blowing your budget on stuff you probably don't even need.

Plus, before you know it, you're drowning in debt. Those payments start piling up, along with fees and interest if you pay late or miss a payment, turning a small purchase into a big financial headache. Suddenly, your carefully planned budget goes out the window and you're left scrambling to cover unexpected expenses.

And let's be real, when you're stuck paying off debt you didn't plan for, it eats into your budget for things you actually want to do. No matter how hard you worked on your budget, BNPL can derail your financial plans.

In my opinion, there are better alternatives to BNPL – for instance, saving up for items you want, and setting up a guilt-free savings account that you can fund and replenish.

The Era of Influencers

Talking about debt is not complete without addressing the impact influencers can have on your finances. I mean, who doesn't have a bunch of social media stars they love following? I sure do! But here's the thing: it's so easy to get sucked into buying stuff they promote, especially when their pictures and videos make it all look so incredible. Trust me, I get it.

Lots of influencers use their platforms to showcase products and services, aiming to persuade their audience to make a purchase. And in return, brands pay them for promoting these items. From clothing and makeup hauls to handbag and shoe unboxings, to reviews of kitchen products and educational tools, there's an influencer for everything.

Sometimes, they're sharing products they truly use and adore, which can be super-helpful when you're seeking recommendations. But there are also times when they're just promoting stuff to make a quick buck. Either way, it's crucial to be mindful of the influence they have over you and your finances.

Getting too wrapped up in influencers and their promotions can leave you feeling discontent with what you already have, making you feel like you absolutely need what they're selling. This in turn can cause you to impulse spend, derail your budget, and even rack up unnecessary debt.

It's easy to get swept up in the excitement of buying the same things as your favorite influencers but it's also important to consider how much time you're spending on influencer content.

Don't be afraid to unsubscribe from or unfollow influencers whose content you find is having a negative impact on your finances. Keeping track of your social media time and setting limits can also help you be more aware of what you're consuming and where your money is going. Consider setting reminders to check in on your financial goals and budget, trying out a new hobby, or even deleting your payment info from your browser and social accounts to keep you focused on your goals.

Getting Ready to Pay Down Your Debt

While it's easy to get overwhelmed if you have a ton of debt to pay, the good news is that by changing your spending habits and reprioritizing your finances, you can pay your debt off and have peace of mind.

Here are some key actions that will assist you on your journey to becoming debt free:

1. **Get radical about your debt.** Make a mental commitment to get rid of your debt ASAP. Think of it as a do-or-die matter – you need it out of your life immediately and under no circumstances should you apply for any new debt.
2. **Write it all down.** Visual representation of your debt is the most important step. This will give you an overview of all your debt in one place. Gather all your credit card statements, overdrafts, and loan statements and write down the amount you owe for each one of these items along with their associated interest rate.

   At this point, it's also important to differentiate between good debt and bad. An example of good debt is a mortgage: a home is an asset that could potentially appreciate in value over the long term, despite the ups and downs of the real estate market. At the very least, if you pay off your mortgage, you'll end up owning your home outright.

   An example of bad debt is your credit card: this is a liability. You've spent the money – it's gone – and you are left paying high interest on an item that's probably not doing anything for you or you don't even remember.

   Keep in mind, though, that debt is still debt. Good and bad debts are still liabilities you'll have to pay eventually.

You are just prioritizing by moving the good debt to the bottom of your payoff list and putting the bad debt at the top.

3. **Put your list where you can see it every day.** There's nothing like a jolt back to reality when you've bought the latest designer shoes and your debt is staring right in your face on your bathroom mirror when you're getting ready to go out. Having your debt listed in a place where you see it every day will keep your mind on track.
4. **Cut up those credit cards.** So now you have your list written and posted in a place you'll see it all the time. Why are those credit cards still in your wallet? You don't need them. If you can't bear cutting them up, put them in a plastic bag, fill it up with water, and put that bag in the freezer until you've paid each one of them off, never to be used again.
5. **Create a debt repayment strategy.** Having a debt repayment strategy in place will guide you in paying off your debt as quickly as possible while minimizing the amount of interest you pay over the life of that debt. The debt snowball or debt avalanche methods are excellent strategies to use. (You'll learn more about them in the next part of this chapter.)
6. **Create an emergency fund.** As you pay off your debt, you should also start building a small emergency fund. Save $50–$100 from each paycheck until you get to $1000, so that if something comes up, instead of turning to a credit card and adding to your existing debt load, you can turn to your savings, and deal with your emergency.

TIP

It's normal to feel a range of emotions, including frustration or impatience, especially as you get serious about your debt. In order to boost your morale and stay motivated, be sure to

celebrate your wins, like paying off a credit card or sticking to your budget for the month. It's all about focusing on the progress you're making, no matter how small, and avoiding self-criticism or guilt about past financial decisions.

PAYING OFF YOUR DEBT

When it comes to paying off your debt, you need to have a strategy in place that will help you pay it off as quickly as possible. The two most popular strategies are the debt snowball method and the debt avalanche method. Here's how you can use them to your advantage.

The Debt Snowball Method

The debt snowball method is a debt payoff strategy where you pay off multiple credit card balances by starting with the smallest balances first, regardless of interest rate. You pay as much as you can toward that small balance while paying the minimum payment on your larger debts.

Once that first small balance is gone, you take that payment and combine it with the minimum payment on the next smallest balance and you keep going that way until you are making a giant snowball payment against your largest debt, and that debt eventually gets paid off.

Here's a simple example. Let's say you have four debts of \$6000, \$3000, \$2000, and \$500, for a total of \$11,500. With the debt snowball method, your plan would be to pay off the smallest debt first, regardless of the interest rate, so you would order them accordingly:

Debt 1: $500 ($50 minimum payment)
Debt 2: $2000 ($65 minimum payment)
Debt 3: $3000 ($70 minimum payment)
Debt 4: $6000 ($165 minimum payment)

Now, you determine that you can afford to pay $800 toward your total debt each month, based on your budget. In month one, you would start by paying the minimum payments on Debts 2–4. Then the rest of your debt payoff funds would go toward paying down Debt 1. So you would pay the minimum payment plus an additional $450.

By month two, you would have paid off Debt 1. You then continue paying the minimum payments to Debts 3 and 4. The rest of your funds will now go toward paying down Debt 2. You would continue to follow this process until you've paid off Debt 4 in full.

	Payoff total	Minimum amount due	Amount toward next debt	Amount owed after this month			
				Debt 1	Debt 2	Debt 3	Debt 4
Month 1	800	350	450	$500	$2000	$3000	$6000
Month 2	800	350	450	$0	$1935	$2930	$5835
Month 3	800	300	500	$0	$1370	$2860	$5670
Month 4	800	300	500	$0	$805	$2790	$5505
Month 5	800	300	500	$0	$240	$2720	$5340
Month 6	800	300	500	$0	$0	$2325	$5175
Month 7	800	235	565	$0	$0	$1690	$5010
Month 8	800	235	565	$0	$0	$1055	$4845
Month 9	800	235	565	$0	$0	$420	$4680
Month 10	800	235	565	$0	$0	$0	$4300
Month 11	800	235	565	$0	$0	$0	$3500
Month 12	800	165	635	$0	$0	$0	$2700
Month 13	800	165	635	$0	$0	$0	$1900
Month 14	800	165	635	$0	$0	$0	$1100
Month 15	800	165	635	$0	$0	$0	$300
Month 16	800	165	635	$0	$0	$0	$0

Note: This is a simplified example and does not account for reduced minimum payments as debts are paid down.

It works because as human beings, many of us thrive on and get motivated by quick wins. So paying off the smallest balances first, regardless of interest rate, will help you make quick progress and will motivate you to attack the rest of your debt.

The Debt Avalanche Method

The debt avalanche method is where you pay off your debt with the highest interest rate first, regardless of the size of the balance. The process then continues from there.

This plan will save you money in the long run as compared with the debt snowball method. That's because you pay off your high-interest debts first, reducing the amount of interest you pay overall. The drawback is that your first win might take some time.

For example, let's say you have four debts totaling $28,500, broken down as follows:

$10,000 at 15% interest

$9500 at 7% interest

$7000 at 12% interest

$2000 at 5% interest

With the avalanche method, your plan would be to pay off the debt with the highest interest rate first, so you would order them accordingly:

Debt 1: $10,000 at 15% interest ($250 minimum payment)
Debt 2: $7000 at 12% interest ($195 minimum payment)
Debt 3: $9500 at 7% interest ($180 minimum payment)
Debt 4: $2000 at 5% interest ($50 minimum payment)

You've determined that you can pay $1000 toward your debt each month, so, similar to the snowball method, you would pay the minimum payments on Debts 2–4, then you would pay the minimum payment plus whatever is left over (in this case, $325) toward Debt 1. Your repayment would go as follows:

	Payoff total	Minimum amount due	Amount toward next debt	Amount owed after this month			
				Debt 1	Debt 2	Debt 3	Debt 4
Month 1	1000	675	325	$10,000	$7000	$9500	$2000
Month 2	1000	675	325	$9550	$6875	$9375	$1958
Month 3	1000	675	325	$9094	$6749	$9250	$1916
Month 4	1000	675	325	$8633	$6621	$9124	$1874
Month 5	1000	675	325	$8166	$6492	$8997	$1832
Month 6	1000	675	325	$7693	$6362	$8870	$1790
Month 7	1000	675	325	$7214	$6231	$8742	$1747
Month 8	1000	675	325	$6729	$6098	$8613	$1705
Month 9	1000	675	325	$6239	$5964	$8483	$1662
Month 10	1000	675	325	$5741	$5829	$8352	$1619
Month 11	1000	675	325	$5238	$5692	$8221	$1575
Month 12	1000	675	325	$4729	$5554	$8089	$1532
Month 13	1000	675	325	$4213	$5415	$7956	$1488
Month 14	1000	675	325	$3690	$5274	$7823	$1445
Month 15	1000	675	325	$3162	$5132	$7688	$1401
Month 16	1000	675	325	$2626	$4988	$7553	$1356
Month 17	1000	675	325	$2084	$4843	$7417	$1312
Month 18	1000	675	325	$1535	$4696	$7280	$1268
Month 19	1000	425	575	$979	$4548	$7143	$1223
Month 20	1000	425	575	$416	$4399	$7004	$1178
Month 21	1000	425	575	$0	$4094	$6865	$1133
Month 22	1000	425	575	$0	$3365	$6725	$1088
Month 23	1000	425	575	$0	$2629	$6585	$1042
Month 24	1000	425	575	$0	$1885	$6443	$996
Month 25	1000	425	575	$0	$1134	$6301	$951
Month 26	1000	425	575	$0	$375	$6157	$905
Month 27	1000	425	575	$0	$0	$5622	$858
Month 28	1000	230	770	$0	$0	$4705	$812

	Payoff total	Minimum amount due	Amount toward next debt	Amount owed after this month			
				Debt 1	Debt 2	Debt 3	Debt 4
Month 29	1000	230	770	$0	$0	$3783	$765
Month 30	1000	230	770	$0	$0	$2855	$718
Month 31	1000	230	770	$0	$0	$1921	$671
Month 32	1000	230	770	$0	$0	$983	$624
Month 33	1000	230	770	$0	$0	$38	$577
Month 34	1000	230	770	$0	$0	$0	$0

Note: This is a simplified example and does not account for reduced minimum payments as debts are paid down.

Keep in mind that this can be a much tougher approach when compared to the snowball method, especially if your highest-interest debt is associated with your highest balances. There won't be any quick wins using this method. In the example above, it would take 20 months to pay off the first debt – that's a long time before you see any solid results.

TIP

When considering the snowball versus the avalanche debt payoff methods, choose the approach that aligns best with your personality. If you prefer quick wins and motivational boosts, the snowball method may be best because you'll see your debt eliminated faster. On the other hand, if you want to minimize the total amount of interest you pay over time, the avalanche method would be more effective since it targets your highest interest debt first.

Debt Consolidation

When you decide you're ready to start paying back all your debts, you may feel overwhelmed having so many bills to pay at once. Maybe you're feeling confused and mixed up over all the different credit card statements. One way to avoid this issue is to consolidate (combine) that debt into one monthly payment. You can do this by transferring the balances of your different credit cards to a single credit card that has a 0% or very low introductory interest rate.

These low interest rates usually apply for a limited period of time, so it only makes sense if you can pay off your outstanding debt within the timeframe of that introductory rate. You also need to ensure that you carefully read the fine print, so you are aware of any fees associated with the balance transfer. Review everything to make sure the cost of the transfer makes sense.

There are also various organizations that offer debt consolidation services for a small monthly fee. They will call your creditors to negotiate lower interest rates for you and create a payoff timeline for you to follow. If you want to save yourself the monthly fee, call your creditors and negotiate your interest rates yourself. Otherwise, I would suggest you stick to the original plan of paying off each credit card one by one, using one of the methods outlined above.

Calling your creditors to negotiate lower interest rates and creating a payoff plan for yourself might be hard, but being debt free is worth it. Not only will you have more money available to you each month, but you will finally be free of the looming problem.

Take Action

Follow the tips in this chapter to get your debt under control:

1. Make the decision to get radical about your debt.
2. Write all your debts and associated interest rates down on paper.
3. Put the list somewhere you can see it every day to keep you focused on your goal.

4. Cut up your credit cards. (Remove the temptation – you can do it!)
5. Establish your emergency fund of $1000 for the time being.
6. Create a debt repayment strategy and use the snowball or avalanche method to pay down your debt.
7. Once your high-interest debt is under control, boost your emergency fund to three to six months of essentials.

STUDENT LOANS: FACTS AND BASICS

I've had countless conversations with family, friends, and colleagues who have student loan debt – anywhere from a few thousand dollars to hundreds of thousands of dollars. From these conversations, I've become all too familiar with the frustrations associated with taking on student loan debt. It seems like student loans are the new normal: if you want to go to college or further your education, student loan debt is part of that package.

A college education is incredibly expensive, and every year those costs go up. As a result, about 70% of college students graduate with an average of $40,000 in debt. Of that 70%, women hold about two-thirds of all U.S. student loan debt, with Black women carrying more student debt on average ($37,558) than other demographics.[2] So if you have student loan debt, you are among the millions of people in the United States who have federal or private student loans.

In my experience, people who have student loans usually fall into one of two categories: they either feel like their student loan debt is so enormous that they will never get out of it, or they simply don't consider their student loans as "bad" debt.

Student loans are also commonly deferred or deprioritized due to their low interest rates (typically lower than the interest

[2] https://www.aauw.org/resources/research/deeper-in-debt

rates associated with credit cards or other debt) and the idea that you have plenty of time to pay them off.

If you fall into either of these categories, it's time to adjust your mindset about your student loans, because they are a real part of your overall debt portfolio. That means that, like your credit cards, you should have a plan to pay off these loans.

I also want you to keep in mind that while $40,000 in student loan debt sounds like a lot, if you are earning an income and you have a plan in place, you can pay off this debt relatively easily. Melisa's story will show you exactly how to make that possible.

MEET MELISA BOUTIN

Melisa successfully paid off over $37,000 of her student loan debt on a limited income while supporting her family. Based on this experience, Melisa is now a Certified Financial Education Instructor (CFEI) and student loan expert who is passionate about filling the gaps when it comes to student loan education. You can find her online at http://yourmoneyworth.com.

As a young college student, you were burdened, like thousands of other women, with a large amount of student loan debt. When did you realize the implications of the debt you had acquired?

> I had an inkling that I was taking on too much debt for college as I got into the second year of my undergraduate studies. I had moved off campus to save on the cost of my attendance, started working two part-time jobs, and carried a full course load – and still had to rely on student loans to get by.
>
> Although I didn't sum up all the debt I had at that point, I knew that continuing to carry the cost of my education for another two years didn't make sense.

> Before the end of my second year in college, I made a plan to change schools to reduce my reliance on student loans. I was able to reduce my costs of attendance significantly, but still ended up with higher than average student loan debt when I graduated.

What challenges did you face once you completed graduate school when trying to find a job that would allow you to pay off the debt? How did you overcome this challenge?

> After college, I continued my education by going to graduate school, and once I finished my master's degree, it took me eight months to find a full-time job in my field of study, which was civil engineering.
>
> During those eight months, I was employed as a census worker, where I earned much less than what I could expect to earn at a job in my field. This resulted in me slowing down my debt payoff. Although I was not able to make full payments on my student loans while I looked for work in my field, I kept track of the interest on my student loans that were in deferment and paid off the interest before it capitalized. Once I found a full-time engineering position, I was able to save thousands on the interest costs for my student loans and accelerate my loan payoff at the same time.

While you were paying off your student loan debt, you were also supporting your family. To what extent was your support and how did you balance that responsibility with paying down your debt?

> I assisted my parents with rent and utility payments, which ranged from $200 to $900 each month. In order to pay down debt while meeting

this obligation, I budgeted my debt payments and reduced my housing costs to less than $500 per month by renting shared housing and living with roommates. In doing this, I was able to help my family and still meet my own financial obligations.

What are some key pieces of advice that every woman needs to know about student loans and paying them off?

Women enroll in college at higher rates than men, but also take on more student loan debt. Women entering college or pursuing a graduate education should always seek to minimize student loan debt on the front end.

That means keeping the maximum student loan debt to less than their expected starting salary after graduation, whether that is through actively pursuing college scholarships, securing employment with education reimbursement benefits, or by choosing an affordable college and program.

Women who have already taken on student loan debt must prioritize managing their personal finances well, reducing their personal finance knowledge gap, avoiding additional consumer debt, and planning their finances around paying off student loan debt quickly.

WHERE TO START WITH YOUR STUDENT LOANS

I've talked to tons of women who are completely overwhelmed by the size of their student loans and don't think it's possible to be free of them until they actually sit down to structure a plan around their debt. Then they have their *aha* moment.

For instance, Kimberly, a member of the Clever Girl Finance Tribe, had just under $30,000 in student debt and was making the suggested minimum payments on her loans. When we talked, she was stressed and felt like she wasn't seeing her principal balance change.

And then there was Jess, who had six figures in student loans from law school and felt that there was no way she would be able to pay off this debt on a public service salary.

What both of these women had in common was a lot of debt but no structured plan in place to tackle it. Once we sat down to come up with a strategy, they started to catch a glimpse of the light at the end of the tunnel.

While they are both still on their debt repayment journeys, they've made massive strides toward becoming student loan debt free. Kimberly has paid off almost half of her student loans and Jess's loans are now under six figures.

All of this is to say that your plan of attack is of utmost importance. It makes all the difference in terms of how quickly you pay off your loans.

As you get into this section and start working on a plan to pay off your student loans, I want you to make up your mind that your student loan debt is not debt that you will have in perpetuity. Like, seriously, you're not here for that. The journey might take a while, but you can get to the other side of your debt with patience and commitment to the process.

Here are some key tips to help you create a strategy to deal with your student loans:

1. **Be aware of all your student loans and the terms and conditions associated with them.** A lot of young college students sign paperwork they don't quite understand or even remember. In fact, a lot of people don't even know how much they owe and to whom they owe it. If you're in that category, don't worry. Your student loans are recorded on your credit report. If you need the details of your loans, order a free copy of your report today (you can get one at http://annualcreditreport.com) and make sure you know what you owe and to whom.

Once you're aware of all these details, you can create a proper plan around your debt and significantly improve your chances of repayment. Plus, you won't have to deal with surprise debt and interest you didn't realize you owed.

In the process of figuring out the details of your debt, get a copy of your promissory note. Review it to ensure you are aware of the information it contains about the terms and conditions of your loan, including:

- The interest rates on your loans and types of loans you have (Are the interest rates fixed or variable?)
- The interest accrual period
- The details of any in-school, deferment, forbearance, repayment, and postgraduate grace periods
- Your student loan capitalization date (unpaid interest added to your principal balance before your first payment is due)
- Any loan fees, late charges, and collection fees
- How payments on your student loan account will be applied (i.e. how much goes to your principal and how much goes to interest)

2. **Factor your student loan payments into your budget and pay more than the minimum.** In addition to paying off your credit card or high-interest debt, your student loans should be on your priority list. The one good thing about student loan debt (if you can call it a good thing) is that interest rates are typically lower than most other types of debt.

   You'll want to make sure your weekly or monthly budget includes your minimum student loan payments plus any extra you can afford to add on each month. Having these loans built into your budget will help you determine if you have any spare money in your budget to apply toward knocking down your principal amounts.

3. **Prioritize your student loan payments.** Depending on the interest rates and the terms surrounding your student loans, you can create a priority list to determine which of your loans you'll focus on paying off first. You might choose to focus on paying off the ones with the highest interest rate first or the ones with the highest balance first, or perhaps the ones with the least flexible loan terms. Look back to the snowball and avalanche methods of debt repayment for this part.

   Federal student loans usually have lower interest rates than private loans, so you should try to tackle your private loans first if you have both types.

4. **Make sure all your additional payments are being applied to your loan principal.** If you are making more than the minimum payments on your student loans (go you!), make sure your additional payments are being applied to your principal and not to the interest. Otherwise, you'll never see your balances go down. Many creditors will apply your payments to interest by default, so double check with them.

   Be sure to review your statements, log in to your accounts, and, if necessary, call your creditors to ensure your additional payments are going toward your principal.

5. **Don't skip your student loan payments.** Skipping loan payments just adds to the time it will take to repay and the interest you will have to pay. A lot of times when you graduate, you have a postgraduation grace period that will allow you to skip payments for a certain amount of time, theoretically while you find a job. However, if you don't have to defer your payments, do not do it. Start making payments as early as you can.

6. **Look into student loan forgiveness programs and employee benefit programs.** If you are still in school or you've gone back for grad school, don't wait until you

graduate before you start strategizing your student loan payoff. One smart approach is to research student loan forgiveness programs that you may be eligible for and ensure that you thoroughly understand their requirements.

The Federal Student Aid website (https://studentaid.ed.gov/sa) provides information on federal forgiveness programs available for federal student loans. That would be a good place to start. Keep in mind, however, that the federal government is not the only one in the student loan forgiveness business. Make sure to research loan forgiveness programs at the state and local level as well.

When it comes to employee benefits, some employers offer student loan repayment benefits as a perk. Be sure to inquire about this and take full advantage if your employer can make this available to you.

7. **Don't stop saving for your future self.** Once you have a plan in place for your student loans, don't stop saving for your future self. Pay yourself first, even if it means contributing just a small percentage of your income to your retirement savings while you focus on tackling your debt. Also, if your employer offers a match on your retirement contributions, take it. It's essentially free money and an immediate 100% return on your contributions. (I'll offer more about this in the next chapter.)

Melisa Boutin, money coach, student loan expert, and the founder of http://yourmoneyworth.com, recommends following these guidelines when it comes to getting your student loans under control:

- Be sure to have your student loan account numbers, initial amount borrowed, and lender information documented.
- Be aware of the start and end of your postgraduation repayment grace period as well as your loan repayment start date.

- Get a copy of your loan amortization schedule and payment information.
- Review every statement you receive and pay close attention to the details around your principal balance and unpaid interest balance.
- Take some time out to review and understand the following:
  - How your payments will be allocated toward fees, interest, and principal
  - Your lender's customer service standards and procedures on delinquency, defaults, and deferments
  - Your lender's options for deferment
  - Your lender's policies and procedures on refinancing and consolidating your loans
- Be sure to set up your online account so you can access your records and payment receipts electronically.

Explore Scholarships

If you are still in school, are planning to pursue an additional degree or certification, or plan to pay for a child's college education, it's worth exploring scholarship options because a wide variety exist. Here are a few examples of scholarship categories you can explore:

- Full-ride scholarships
- Need-based scholarships (based on financial need)
- Merit-based scholarships (based on academic achievement)
- Athletic scholarships
- Minority scholarships
- Creative/performing arts scholarships
- Employer scholarships
- Military scholarships

- Study abroad scholarships
- State or government scholarships

You can find the specifics on these scholarships from various sources, including:

- The financial aid section on the websites of the colleges and universities you are interested in applying to or already attend
- Websites like http://bigfuture.collegeboard.org/scholarship-search, http://Appily.com, http://Fastweb.com, and http://Scholarships.com
- Inquiring about scholarship options from your employers
- Professional associations and organizations related to your career path that provide scholarships to specific fields or industries
- The Federal Student Aid (FAFSA) portal from the U.S. Department of Education for federal scholarships and grants (http://studentaid.gov/understand-aid/types/scholarships)
- Your state government education agency for scholarships specific to your state (http://www2.ed.gov/about/contacts/state)

Take Action

When it comes to getting your student loans under control, be sure to:

- Make time to review the details of your student loans so you are aware of what your loan terms and conditions are.
- Look into any forgiveness programs and employee benefit programs that you may be eligible for.
- Confirm that any additional payments you make will be applied to your principal balance.

- Build your student loan payments (and any additional payments you are able to make) into your budget.
- If you are currently in school, are considering pursuing an additional degree or certification, or are planning to fund a child's college education, make sure to investigate available scholarship options.

IDEAS TO PAY OFF YOUR DEBT FAST

So we've talked about your debt and creating a plan to pay it off, but exactly how can you accelerate that debt repayment? It's all about getting creative and finding ways not just to reduce your expenses but also to increase your income so you have more money to knock out your debt faster.

For the biggest impact, try out a combination of the tips I share in this section. If you stay focused, in a few months you'll be surprised at the difference these small changes will make with paying down your debt.

- **Develop the right money mindset.** When it comes to tackling your debt, having a positive mindset is super-important. It's like giving yourself a pep talk and believing that you've got what it takes to crush that debt. It might take some time, so being mentally prepared is key. Tell yourself things like "I've got this," "Being debt-free is awesome," and "Peace out, debt!" on an ongoing basis. But remember, it's not just about saying these things; you have to really believe in them too.
- **Consolidate your debt into lower interest rate payments.** As I mentioned earlier, a good idea might be to consolidate your debt into one monthly payment by transferring the balances from your current credit cards to a new single credit card that has a 0% or very low introductory interest rate.

For some people, having a single consolidated payment helps them better manage their debt payoff. A lower interest rate will reduce the amount of total interest you pay to your creditors. However, debt consolidation only makes sense if you can pay off your debt within the time frame of the low introductory rate – you don't want to get stuck with all your debt on a high-interest card! You also want to make sure to read the fine print very carefully so you understand the fees and terms associated with transferring your balance.

- **Pay more than the minimum.** As I've already mentioned, paying more than the minimum will save you money on monthly interest payments and accelerate how quickly you become debt free. So make it a goal of yours to pay as much as you can each month toward your credit card debt. You'll speed up your repayment and reduce the amount of overall interest you pay to your creditors.

  It might mean a tighter budget over the short term, but once your debt is gone, you can then reassign that money to your other goals.

- **Use nonretirement or nonemergency savings.** Do you have cash that's sitting in a savings account earning little or no interest? Well, you might want to consider using those funds to pay down your credit card debt.

  All it takes is stepping back and taking a look at your overall financial picture. If you find that the interest you are paying on your credit cards far exceeds the interest rates you're earning on your savings account, it makes mathematical sense to pay down your debt.

  Once your debt is paid off, you can put the money you would have otherwise been using for credit card payments back toward your savings to build it up again.

  Just remember, always keep your retirement and emergency savings intact. The last thing you want is to have to go back into debt if something unexpected comes up.

- **Sell stuff you no longer use.** A quick way to make some extra cash is by getting rid of electronics, clothing, shoes, and accessories you've never worn or no longer use. You can sell your items online on sites like eBay or at a local consignment store. Be sure to price your items competitively and review the feedback from potential buyers very carefully before you sell. Once you get that cash, you can apply it directly to your debt.
- **Ask for a raise.** If you've been at your job for a while and think you are due for raise, it's worth having the conversation with your boss to ask for one. Once that raise comes through, you'll want to funnel it directly toward your debt payoff.
- **Start a side hustle.** Do you have a particular skill set that people compliment you on all the time? Or do you have a strong interest in a particular thing? Then maybe it's time you start charging for those skills to earn some extra income. Baking, crafting, graphic design, freelance work – whatever it is, earn some money with your talents and apply it to your debt.
- **Get a part-time job.** If running your own side hustle is not your cup of tea, you can consider getting a temporary part-time job until your debts are paid off. Be sure to remind yourself why you are working the extra hours – to get rid of your debt. This is only temporary and will totally be worth it in the long run!
- **Cut cable.** Cutting cable can save you a lot of money each month. If you are not an avid sports fan, you might not even miss it at all! Consider switching to an online streaming service like Netflix or Hulu to save some extra cash until your debts are paid off. There's a ton of great content available through streaming services so pick one or two you know you'll watch the most. Remember, your goal is to save money, so avoid subscribing to too many services so you don't end up with a big monthly bill!

- **Lower your cell phone plan.** Cell phone plans can get really expensive, especially when it comes to data. Call your service provider to see if there are any specials or offers they can give you for being a loyal customer. Or consider downgrading your plan to one that costs less or switching to another provider altogether if they offer a cheaper plan. We know you need a phone, so don't cancel it entirely, but you can opt for a minimal plan to save some extra cash that will go toward your debt.
- **Take lunch to work every day.** Eating out every day adds up: the average lunch at a restaurant costs between $10 and $15! Instead, plan your lunches for the week based on what you purchase at the grocery store and what you have at home. Take in leftovers from dinner the night before, or specially prepared meals. Either way, you'll save a ton of money by bringing your own food. Pinterest is a great place to get meal planning ideas if you need help coming up with meal options.
- **Skip the movies and nights out for a while.** Movies and nights out also add up. Rather than spending those nights out, try having a special evening in. Make a special meal with your family, your partner, or your friends instead of eating out. Turn on Netflix and pick something exciting instead of popping by the theater.

  Don't want to give up going out? Skip the ridiculously priced popcorn and beverages at the movies and the alcohol on nights out. These items are heavily marked up, and you can put that money toward your debt instead.
- **Carpool.** If you have coworkers who live nearby, see if you can set up a carpool schedule to save money on gas each week, and put those savings toward your debt.
- **Cut down on your grocery spending.** Save a few dollars off your grocery bill that can go toward your debt repayment. The easiest way to save money at the grocery

store is by making sure you have a list before you go, and a full stomach! This way you don't get sidetracked by what you don't need or whatever food cravings pop up while you're there. Also, check to see what coupons and sales your store has before you go, and see if you can find manufacturer coupons as well.

- **Cancel unused memberships and subscriptions.** Take a look at your finances and see if you're paying monthly fees for things you don't use. If you barely go to the gym or aren't using a particular subscription, cancel it and put those funds toward your debt. If you're worried that getting rid of your gym membership will mean you won't work out, you can always try working out outdoors or with videos on YouTube.
- **Use tax refunds and bonuses to pay off your debt.** Every year, it's almost inevitable that you'll get some form of extra cash. Whether that's a gift card, a tax rebate, your entire tax return, or a bonus at work, use that extra cash to pay down your debt. Those refunds and bonuses can make a huge impact toward accelerating your debt payoff. I know many people use their tax returns and bonuses to treat themselves – and that can be very tempting – but think of how much happier you'll be with no debt.
- **Automate your payments.** Set up automatic transfers for the amount you've budgeted toward paying off your debt. For example, if you can afford an extra $200 per month, set up a $200 automatic payment to speed up reducing your balance. Automating payments helps avoid late fees and keeps you focused on becoming debt-free!
- **Get an accountability buddy.** Having a like-minded accountability partner is also helpful. They'll support you, keep you motivated, and help you stay on track with your debt payoff and savings goals.

Take Action

- Use the suggestions in this section to come up with a list of things you can implement right now and in the near future to accelerate your debt payoff.
- Set timelines to complete them and track your progress.

MEET NASEEMA MCELROY

She's a money coach, debt "slaya," and the founder of http://FinanciallyIntentional.com. Outside of encouraging people to get their financial act together, Naseema is also a mother and labor and delivery nurse. Although she had been making six figures for years, she still struggled with money. She finally realized that she couldn't outearn her financial ignorance and decided to make some serious changes. By shifting her mindset around money and being consistent and intentional, she was able to pay off almost $1,000,000 of debt in under three years.

You paid off nearly $1,000,000 of debt, including your home, student loans, and credit cards, in just three years. How did you do it?

> I had to get intentional about where my money was going. I really didn't have a plan for my money before, so although I earned a lot, I was always broke. I started making progress when I got good at giving my money an assignment on a monthly basis, planning my spending at least a few weeks in advance. I used zero-based budgeting and the debt snowball method, making eliminating debt my number-one financial priority.

One of the things that helped you accelerate your debt repayment was selling your home at a profit. Why

were you compelled to pay off the rest of your debt with that money?

My last few debts represented past mistakes. They weighed heavily on me emotionally, and I couldn't wait to eliminate them from my life. The weight that was lifted with those last payments was tangible: I felt like I could finally breathe.

What advice would you give a young woman facing a mountain of debt, thinking it might be impossible to pay off?

You eat an elephant one bite at a time. It's those small, intentional things we do on a daily basis that snowball to help us reach those seemingly insurmountable goals. Set a goal and set a plan of attack (debt snowball, avalanche, or whatever works). If you stick to it long enough, it becomes automatic. Make as many things automated as possible with your finances. It's all about getting started, and today is a great day to start!

How has your life changed now that you are 100% debt free?

I am not quite 100% debt free as I chose to buy my dream car, making a very intentional decision to finance a small portion that I will be paying off soon. I could have paid cash for it, but instead I made a conscious decision to invest in myself and optimize my year-end tax deductions. The most important change is that now every decision I make with money is intentional. I have total control of my money and now use it as a tool to live life on my terms.

> I have a goal that by the time I'm 40 (in three years), I will have enough money saved that working will be optional. I want to be able to travel the world and focus on building experiences with my family. Of course, I'm going to keep sharing my story and letting anyone who will listen know that if this girl out of West Oakland can achieve financial independence, anyone can.

CASHBACK AND REWARDS CREDIT CARDS

When it comes to credit cards, a lot of people opt for cashback or rewards credit cards as a way to get something back when they spend money. It's a nice perk to have, especially if you actually use the rewards you get. However, it can be a slippery slope if you are not careful about how you use them. We'll get into that in this section, but first let me explain the difference between the two.

Cashback Versus Rewards Credit Cards

Cashback and rewards credit cards are based on the same idea – you get something back when you spend money using your credit card.

The main difference between the two is that with cashback you get a percentage of the money you spend on a specific category (e.g. 2% on gas, 1% on groceries). With rewards cards you get some form of points or gift cards. Basically, cashback cards will give you cash, and rewards cards will give you non-cash benefits.

Why give away free money?

The thing about cashback and rewards credit cards is that, while they are a perk for the cardholder, they are also a strategy that credit card companies use to get their cardholders to spend more money.

If you are motivated by an incentive like cashback, you are more likely to shift your focus to wanting to obtain as much of the incentive as possible, which can lead to overspending, especially on low-cost items. This strategy is beneficial to credit card companies because it allows them to make money from interest accrued on credit card balances you can't pay off.

If you are one of those people carrying a balance on your credit card from month to month, then you actually lose out big-time because, despite the incentive you've gained, you are paying way more than it's worth in accrued interest.

How to Use Cashback and Rewards Credit Cards to Your Benefit

When it comes to using a credit card that offers rewards for your day-to-day transactions, it's important to plan out your spending by using a budget. This way, you know exactly how much you can afford to spend in order to pay your balance off in full each month. And you can resist the temptation to overspend just to get cashback or reward points that you could end up paying for in interest later on.

Some credit card companies offer an additional incentive with their cashback cards by advertising 0% interest for an introductory period of time. Before you take them up on that offer, be sure to ask about annual fees and what the interest rate will be after the introductory period. Chances are, if you carry a balance from month to month, once the introductory period is over, you'll be paying back those rewards and then some.

So if you're using cashback or reward credit cards, be mindful of how you use them, and make it a goal to pay off your balance in full each month if you do. The best strategy for these card types is to find one card that offers some benefit but that has no fee associated. Use it only for purchases you would normally make, and then you can use your rewards for a nice treat once in a while.

Take Action

If you have a cashback or rewards credit card, make sure you're making the best of the benefits you receive:

1. Be sure to find the right type of card with a reward that suits your lifestyle. For example, if you travel a lot, a rewards card with miles or travel upgrades might be a great option for you.
2. Be aware of the timeline and expiration around which your rewards or cashback can be redeemed. Use the rewards within that timeframe so you don't miss out.
3. Avoid carrying a balance on these cards and be mindful of your spending when you use them. Always defer to your budget to make sure you're staying on track.

MEET MONICA LOUIE

Monica is a Facebook ads strategist who runs http://FlourishingImpact.com and helps ambitious online entrepreneurs grow their impact and profits by harnessing the power of Facebook ads. Before Monica become her own boss helping other people build wealth by leveraging small business, Monica and her husband were $120,000 in debt and wanted to get out of debt after being inspired by other success stories. Not only did they pay off their debt, but they did it in two short years – and Monica details exactly how they did it.

You and your husband paid off $120,000 in debt in just two years without making six figures. What was the catalyst behind setting this huge goal?

> My husband and I set a huge goal to pay off all of our debt, including our mortgage. At the time, we had around $320,000 in total. We wanted to pay that off by the time we turned 40, which was about eight years away.

The main motivation for setting this huge goal was that I had just become a stay-at-home mom and had another baby on the way. We had some money saved up but were trying to be smart about our financial situation. We wanted to pay off debt and save some extra money in order to provide a buffer for ourselves.

Even though we voluntarily decided to go from two incomes to one with a growing family, we wanted to make smart financial choices. Within the first couple of months, we saw that the amount in our savings was slowly starting to dip, and this made us a bit nervous.

We felt very vulnerable, so we started looking for ways to manage our money better. We knew it was going to involve budgeting and saving and living within our means. On the journey to figuring out how we could manage our money better, we came across various success stories of people who paid off tons of debt. One story in particular was from a family very similar to ours, with a single income and young kids. They had paid off all their debt, including their mortgage, within 10 years!

When I heard that story, I got super-excited because I was imagining doing the same thing and what life would be like if we didn't owe anyone any money.

I did some quick math in my head and added up all our debt – that included our student loans, mortgage, and home equity line of credit.

I knew we were paying more than $2000 per month toward debt. We could do other things with that money, like save more for retirement or our kids' college fund, or even take family vacations without feeling guilty.

How did you and your husband get on the same page around this goal?

> In the beginning, what really got me excited was imagining a life without debt! When I shared the idea with my husband, he was completely onboard. We decided that not only were we going to get a handle on our money, but we were going to attack our debt.
>
> We knew that other people had been able to do it in a similar situation, so we could too! We weren't sure how yet, but we saw the light at the end of the tunnel and had hope that we could accomplish our goal and feel a sense of freedom.
>
> My husband has always been the more frugal one in the relationship. He actually brought savings with him into our marriage! It made him a little bit nervous because I'm a natural spender, and he thought I might blow through his savings. I had to build up trust with him and prove that I was going to be responsible with my spending.
>
> When I was the one to come up with the idea of getting out of debt, he was totally onboard and super-excited to join me on this journey! It made him feel more at peace with transitioning to a single income knowing that we were going to be getting rid of our debt.

What frame of mind did you have while paying off all this debt?

> We never once stopped to think whether paying off the $320,000 of debt in eight years was a realistic goal. We have a bit of a competitive streak and knew that if someone else could do it, then we could too.

We were going to shoot to pay off our debt by the time we turned 40, but we weren't going to be upset if it took a little bit longer than that.

In order to build up momentum and keep going for the long haul – considering this could take more than eight years to complete – we decided to make as much progress as we could as fast as we could. In the first month of our plan, we had a very successful garage sale where we made nearly $1600. We sold my husband's car, which brought in a good amount of money, and then replaced it with a cheaper one.

We also took some of the savings we had built up in preparation for transitioning to a single income and put that toward my husband's student loan. It had a balance of $13,000, and we were able to pay off the entire debt immediately. This helped us feel like we had a big win under our belt within the first month!

Going forward, we continued to look at everything in our house and asked ourselves if we wanted to keep it or try to sell it to make some extra money to pay off debt. Anything we weren't super-attached to was put in a garage sale or posted online. Not everything sold, but every little bit added up in the end!

We decided to get rid of every single thing we could and make some extra money along the way. We cleaned out our garage, closets, cupboards, everywhere! We got rid of anything we no longer needed. Later on, we even sold my husband's motorcycle and a big weight set that was taking up space in our house. These were bigger-ticket items that brought in extra money, but lots of the little things we sold added up quickly too.

One thing we did that kept our momentum up is that I created a very detailed budget. I tracked every dollar and made sure that all of the extra money that was coming in was actually helping to pay down the debt. I was also tracking our debt balances every single month. I tracked how much debt we started with and the growing total that we had paid off every month.

Note that we didn't just track how much debt we paid off that month, but we also tracked the cumulative amount we paid down since starting our debt-free journey. Even to this day, I look back at how much total debt we've paid off. Focusing on that larger number allows us to see that we've made a lot of progress, even during months when we were only able to pay the minimum amount due.

We certainly weren't perfect, though. There were times when we got off track and blew our budget for eating out or bought things we didn't really need. But we didn't let ourselves get discouraged when that happened. We kept going. We reminded ourselves of our goal and thought about how it would feel to be debt free. We focused on the benefit of what we could do when we were debt free and what that new lifestyle would look like. That was what fueled us and kept us moving forward each month!

What advice would you give a couple working on facing their financial challenges together?

My husband and I focused on achieving this huge goal together. We knew that it was a team effort! And it's a goal we're still working on together as a couple. I'm still tracking the money and my husband continues to work overtime at his job. He's also in charge of selling items on online and setting up our garage sales.

It's really been a team effort. This has actually brought us closer together with our money, and we feel like we're striving to achieve this huge goal together. It's something that has really strengthened our relationship as a couple!

My advice for other couples is to look at the positives and to envision what your situation will look like. Focus on how you'll feel once you overcome this financial hurdle together! Then, keep this picture very clear in your mind and put it at the forefront of your decisions together. Keep your eyes on the end result and what reaching this goal will allow you to do.

Also, think about how you can hold each other accountable to your goals and commitments throughout this time. Staying accountable to one another has been a huge part of our process! If one of us wants to go out to eat, the other helps rein us in. When one of us wants to make an impulse purchase, the other can keep them on track and remind them of those shared goals. Doing this means that each partner can balance the other out. You keep each other in check and remind one another of the outcome you're working toward. And don't forget to look back at your progress to see how far you've come together!

Finally, read other people's success stories and be inspired by financial goals that other people have accomplished in a similar situation as you and your partner. You can find lots of success stories online or join other financial communities who can help give you tips and motivation for moving forward.

CHAPTER 5

Investing

Investing is how you grow your money to build long-term wealth!

#CLEVERGIRLSKNOW

INVESTING 101

When it comes to building wealth, investing is my absolute favorite part because this is how your money really grows. Investing is how the wealthy build and maintain their wealth – and you should want to do the same.

When I first started saving money after college, I had no idea about how investing in the stock market worked. The investing world felt like one full of complexities and it was utterly confusing to even watch the financial news. However, I realized quickly that if I was serious about building wealth, I was going to have to learn it and so I began to educate myself by reading books (think *Investing for Dummies*), reading blog posts and articles, and putting what I learned into practice.

As time went on, I realized it wasn't as complicated as I'd made it out be, especially after learning my style as an investor and clearly understanding my investment objectives. That being said, you can learn how to invest and become successful at it too.

If you've ever wondered how you can get started with investing in the stock market, you're in luck. I'll be breaking it all down in this next section. But first, let's start with why it's important.

Note: Although there are other ways to invest your money, like real estate or business, this section will focus on investing as it relates to the stock market.

What Investing Is and Why It's Important

Like I mentioned earlier, investing is how you grow your money. Putting money into a savings account is great for the short term (i.e. for things like your emergency fund or saving for a house down payment), or money you need easily accessible or will need within five or so years.

However, for the long term (for instance, retirement), investing your money is the way to go, especially given the very low interest rates on savings accounts. At less than 1% average savings interest in the United States, you are basically making no money! So investing in the stock market, which has an average rate of return of about 8%, will make you much more money in the long run. But that's not all! When you add on the power of compounding, we are talking about a potentially large nest egg with consistent investing.

How Compounding Works

The concept of compounding is probably one of the more complex aspects of investing – and to be honest, it's not that complicated! Compounding is the process by which your money grows from reinvesting your earnings over time. Basically, when you earn interest on your investment, rather than taking out that money, it gets added on to your balance only to earn interest on itself. Over the course of many years, compounding really adds up!

Let's look at a very basic example. Let's say you invest $1000 at 10% interest. At the end of one year, you'll have $1100.

If you leave the $1100 in your account and don't even put any other money into your investment the next year, at the end of year two, you will have earned an additional $110 for an overall total of $1210. Over several years, it adds up nicely.

Take a look at this comparison chart to see how compounding can be beneficial.

Initial investment	$1000.00
Year 1	$1100.00
Year 2	$1210.00
Year 3	$1331.00
Year 4	$1464.10
Year 5	$1610.51
Year 6	$1771.56
Year 7	$1948.72
Year 8	$2143.59

Year 9	$2357.95
Year 10	$2593.74
Year 11	$2853.12
Year 12	$3138.43
Year 13	$3452.27
Year 14	$3797.50
Year 15	$4177.25
Year 16	$4594.97
Year 17	$5054.47
Year 18	$5559.92
Year 19	$6115.91
Year 20	$6727.50
Year 21	$7400.25
Year 22	$8140.27
Year 23	$8954.30
Year 24	$9849.73
Year 25	$10,834.71

In 25 years, you'd earn $9834.71 on your initial $1000 investment, even if you never put any other money into that account again. Compare that to the $2500 ($100 multiplied by 25 years) you would have made without compounding.

Key Investing Concepts

Now that you understand how compounding works, you're well on your way to getting your head around investing. But before we go any further, there are some key investing concepts that you'll need to know.

Your Investment Objectives

Your objectives are essentially tied to why you are investing and how long your investment term is likely to be. For instance, saving for retirement or saving for your kids' college education are examples of long-term investment objectives that require a considerable amount of money to achieve. On the other hand, investing to buy a car would be a short-term objective that will require relatively less. Having clear objectives and clear timeframes will also help you create a sound investing plan and help you make the best decisions about which stocks and funds you want to be involved with.

For example, based on when you'd like to retire, you can plan to make your retirement portfolio more conservative as you approach your retirement date. Doing this will ensure that, if there is a market decline around the time you retire, your investments are protected, and you can stay on course with your plan.

As a rule, you don't want to invest any money in the stock market that you have allocated for short-term goals or goals you want to accomplish within five years or fewer. Why? Well, the stock market is hard to predict, so a lot of volatility can happen over the short term. Investing for the long term (the longer the better) allows you to weather short-term market declines or volatility.

Rates of Return

In investing, *returns* are the profits you make on your investments. The *rate of return* (RoR) is the average profit the investment achieves (or is expected to achieve) over a specified time period and is usually depicted as a percentage.

As you look at different kinds of investments, you'll find that one of the data points tied to each investment is the RoR. With some research, you'll be able to see what the historical RoR is on any investment and, if it has been around long enough, you'll also be able to see how they did in both good and bad economic conditions.

You can also use the RoR as a data point when comparing different investment options.

Risk and Risk Tolerance

With every investment comes a degree of risk – this is why it's really important that you understand your risk tolerance as an investor. In other words, you'll want to ask yourself how much risk you can stomach, keeping in mind that higher rates of return are typically associated with higher risk.

One way to gauge your risk tolerance is to take a look at your investment objectives and how much time you have to reach them. If they are several years away, you might be able to give yourself more room to take on risk, but if they are coming up in a few years, you might want to focus on staying conservative.

Also, your level of experience with investing is a factor to consider when it comes to taking on risk and your risk tolerance. If you are a newbie investor who is still getting comfortable with how the stock market works, it's best to go conservative. However, if you are experienced and comfortable with how it all works, you can likely tolerate more risk.

The risk factor, also known as *risk profile*, is another data point commonly associated with different investments in the stock market and can guide you as you make decisions on what to invest in.

Economic Cycles

Over time, every economy goes through cycles as it grows or expands and then declines or contracts. Investments in the stock market are directly impacted by what part of an economic cycle the economy is experiencing. For instance, in a recession where there are fewer jobs and people are more mindful of how they spend their disposable income, stock prices can experience declines. On the other hand, as we go through periods of expansion, stock prices are more likely to increase.

Basic Investing Terms

In addition to the key investing concepts you should know, you also want to make sure that you are aware of the basic terms and lingo associated with investing in the stock market. Understanding how investing works begins with learning the basic, most commonly used investment terms.

Brokerage firm: A brokerage firm is a financial institution that manages or facilitates the buying and selling of securities (different kinds of investments like stocks, bonds, and funds) between buyers and sellers. They typically charge commission fees on trades and can provide you with up-to-date research, market analysis, and pricing information on various securities. Examples of brokerage firms in the United States include Vanguard, Fidelity, Charles Schwab, and T. Rowe Price.

Robo-advisor: A robo-advisor does what a brokerage firm does but at a much lower cost. These transactions and bits of advice are mostly based on algorithms with minimal human interactions. Examples include Acorns, Betterment, Wealthfront, and Fidelity Go.

Diversification: In simple terms, diversification means not putting all your eggs in one basket. Instead, you put your money in a mix of investments to minimize your overall risk.

Prospectus: A prospectus is a legal document filed with the Securities and Exchange Commission (SEC) that provides details of an investment that is made publicly available for sale.

Stock: A stock is part ownership of a company. Stocks are also called shares or equities, and the more you own, the bigger your ownership stake is in a company.

Bond: In simple terms, a bond is a loan you make to a company or the government with the intention of being paid back in full, with interest. For example, the government sells bonds to raise money for a specific initiative. You can purchase the bond and the government will pay you back over a fixed period of time with interest. Bonds typically pay out interest at regular intervals and are traded in the bond market, as the values of bonds change over time.

Mutual fund: A mutual fund is a pool of money from a group of investors set up for the purpose of buying securities like individual stocks and bonds. Mutual funds are overseen by a fund manager associated with a brokerage firm. Their job is to make investment decisions for the fund and set the fund's objectives. Typically, mutual funds are less risky than individual stocks because they are internally diversified.

Index fund: This is a type of mutual fund with a portfolio constructed to match or track the components of a market index. An index is a series of stocks that are tracked together to give clues as to how the economy is performing. You've probably heard of the Dow Jones or the S&P 500.

So, in plain English, an index fund is set up to buy all the same stocks within a specific index, so your RoR is the same as the change in the index over time. For example, if you invest in an S&P 500 index, you are invested in every single one of the 500 companies that make up that index. As the index goes up, your return increases at the same rate.

Exchange-traded fund: Similar to index funds, exchange-traded funds (ETFs) track an index or a set of securities. However, unlike an index fund or mutual fund, they can be actively traded in the stock market throughout the day at the current market price. Because they can be actively traded throughout the day, brokerage commission fees are charged when you buy and sell.

Bond fund: A bond fund is a type of investment fund that pools money from multiple investors to invest in a diversified portfolio of bonds.

Target date fund: A target date fund is an investment plan that helps you save for a specific future event, like retirement. The fund is structured to adjust gradually over time, starting with more aggressive investments like stocks and gradually moving to more conservative investments like bonds as you get closer to your target date. The fund's name usually tells you the year it's aiming for. For example, "Target Date 2055 Fund" would be for people planning to retire around 2055. They're popular in retirement accounts (e.g. 401ks and IRAs), because they help manage risk and build a diversified portfolio without you having to do much.

Asset allocation: This is essentially how you balance risk by creating a portfolio based on your objectives, risk tolerance, and timeline. Your asset allocation is usually expressed in percentages, as in, you have 50% of your investment in stocks and 50% in bonds.

Capital gains: This is when the value of your investment becomes higher than your original purchase price. In other words, your capital gains are the earnings your investment makes that are not realized until the asset is sold. As an example, if you invest $1000 in a mutual fund and then sell those shares for $1500, your capital gain on that sale is $500. Capital gains are also taxed at a different rate than income, which can be beneficial to you in the long run.

Expense ratio: This is the portion of the assets in a fund that will be used for operating expenses. These include management fees and administrative fees. It's basically the operating costs divided by the total assets in the fund. Note that the expense ratio is a cost and therefore reduces the total assets in the fund over time.

Yield: This is how much you make over a certain period of time with your investment, not including the principal amount.

Benchmark: Think of a benchmark as a yardstick for measuring how well an investment is doing. It's like a standard that tells you if your investment is doing great or not so great. For example, the Dow Jones Industrial Average is a popular benchmark used to track the performance of big, well-known companies.

Dividend: This is a profit share given to the shareholders in a company. It is essentially a thank-you that shareholders receive for owning shares in the company. Dividends are typically paid out regularly, such as quarterly or annually, and they can be in the form of cash or additional shares of stock.

Volatility: This is how much an investment changes value, moving between more and less value. Generally, higher volatility means that you're taking on more risk. With a well-diversified portfolio, you can afford to do this in some cases.

Real estate investment trust (REIT): This is a company that owns or manages large real estate properties that make money (e.g. malls, offices, apartments, hotels, and warehouses) and allows you to make an investment in real estate through them. When you invest in a REIT, you're investing in these properties without having to buy them yourself. It's a way for regular investors to be part of the real estate market without dealing with physical property management. You can purchase shares of publicly traded REITs on the stock exchange or within certain mutual funds and ETFs.

Bull market: A bull market is when the stock market is on the upswing. People are feeling pretty good about the economy and how businesses are doing. Basically, it's a time when stock prices are going up and everyone's feeling optimistic about investing. According to the U.S. Securities and Exchange Commission, we officially call it a bull market when the market rises by 20% or more in broad-based index funds for at least two months.[1]

Bear market: A bear market is the opposite of a bull market. It's when the stock market starts taking a nosedive instead of going up. During a bear market, people tend to feel pretty gloomy about the economy, and they're not as confident about investing in the market. According to the SEC, we officially call it a bear market when the market drops by 20% or more over at least a two-month period.[2]

When it comes to investing in the stock market (or any other avenue, for that matter), remember that past performance of the market is not an indication of future performance, but historical trends do matter because they help you make informed investing decisions.

Investing should be for the long term! I cannot repeat this enough. Investing for the long term allows you to grow your

[1]https://www.investor.gov/introduction-investing/investing-basics/glossary/bull-market

[2]https://www.investor.gov/introduction-investing/investing-basics/glossary/bear-market

portfolio, weather storms, and make gains. While you can trade stocks in the stock market on a daily, monthly, or annual basis, this is not the type of investing that brings you a consistent and reliable increase in your assets. Investing for retirement, on the other hand, is ideal.

Take Action

Spend some time familiarizing yourself with the key investing concepts and basic investing terms mentioned in this section. In addition, if you have current investments with a brokerage firm, through a robo-advisor, or via your employer, do some investigating to determine your investment's historical data, current RoR, and expense ratio or fees.

MEET ADEOLA OMOLE

Adeola is a wealth coach at http://adeolaomole.com and author of *7 Steps to Get Out of Debt and Build Wealth*. Her life's mission is to help educate women about personal finance matters related to money management, investment strategies, and debt management options. She paid off $390,000 in debt, including student loans, car loans, a line of credit, credit cards, and her mortgage, and now has seven figures in assets, which she achieved through strategic investing. Adeola shares insights from her journey to achieving debt freedom and building wealth through investing.

You went from paying off six figures in debt to having seven figures in assets. How exactly did you build your now-positive net worth?

> I paid off over $390,000 of debt in two stages. First, I paid off just over $70,000 of consumer debt in less than three years. Then, over the course of 12 years, I paid off over $320,000 that was owed on my home.

I was able to get rid of this six-figure debt in a reasonable amount of time by implementing a supercharged financial strategy that I created.

Once I paid off my consumer debt, I was able to build my seven-figure net worth. Specifically, I opened up a high-interest savings account that was designated for the purpose of creating wealth. Then I began to fund the account with the money that was previously going toward my monthly debt payments.

I had become accustomed to paying approximately $2800 a month toward my debt, so I didn't miss the money once it was redirected into the account. Accordingly, it was relatively effortless for me to divert the funds into my account. The money in the account grew rapidly and had reached close to $35,000 in the first year.

I began to use the money in the account to build my wealth and to fund investment opportunities. For instance, I paid down my mortgage, purchased stocks and other investments in my brokerage accounts, purchased two rental properties, and used some of the funds to start my own business. I have since sold both rental properties and received close to $200,000 in profits. I continued to grow my net worth by investing in the stock market and in my coaching business.

Getting out of debt was the best financial decision I've made because it opened the door for me to build the life-changing wealth I have today. It is very difficult for those who are mired in debt to believe they can build wealth. However, my journey demonstrates that it is absolutely possible.

What was your motivation for wanting to become financially successful?

When I was in my mid-20s, I had just lost my job as a lawyer and was terrified about my financial future. At the time, I was drowning in debt, had a negative net worth, and was living paycheck to paycheck. To put it bluntly, I was afraid that I would have to file for bankruptcy and might lose my home. I made a vow to myself to find a way to get rid of all the debt, so I would never have to answer to a creditor again. I had to learn the hard way that my Visa was not my emergency fund.

After trying to get a credit limit increase on my Visa and being declined, I reached my financial rock bottom. It was at this point that I vowed to never rely on a creditor for my financial well-being. My motivation was to attain financial freedom so I would never have to rely on a creditor or employer for my financial future. I vowed to take my financial destiny into my own hands.

What does it feel like now knowing you are financially secure for life, and how are you ensuring it is permanent?

It feels absolutely amazing to be financially secure for life. It's deeply gratifying that I have built a seven-figure net worth that allows me to live my life's purpose and build a legacy for my children. I am also humbled by the fact that I have been able to reach my goal of financial freedom and feel called to teach others how they can achieve the same level of success.

I'm ensuring that my financial security lasts for life by making it a priority to continue to be a prudent investor and to invest wisely in my business. As it relates to my stock market portfolio, I have been able to grow my assets by implementing investment strategies that allow me to buy investments when they are at a deep discount to their intrinsic value and sell investments when they are overvalued. This strategy has helped grow my net worth consistently, year after year. And one valuable lesson I have learned over the years is the importance of having a great strategy in place to reach your financial goals.

The best advice I have for anyone beginning their financial journey is never to lose hope, and to recognize that the clearest path to building wealth begins by paying off your debt. Building life-changing wealth does not happen overnight. It takes time and requires that you establish a financial plan, then execute on that plan. If I was able to amass a seven-figure net worth after having been unemployed for 18 months and in $390,000 of debt, I am confident you will be able to rise out of your financial situation and build life-changing wealth, too!

INVESTING FOR RETIREMENT

When I shared my money story earlier, I talked about investing for retirement and how despite not knowing how it all worked, I chose to take advantage of my employer's match and began automated contributions to my retirement accounts.

Well, within those first three or four years of contributing, my retirement account amassed nearly $40,000 from my contributions, compounding, and market gains, making it a worthwhile decision. While I was successful even though I wasn't sure what I was doing, I know it would have been much more profitable had I made better and smarter choices then.

Given this early experience, I strongly recommend having a plan in place to invest for retirement. For many people, investing for retirement is their first real introduction to investing, but the *what, how,* and *where* of saving for retirement can be quite confusing for someone just getting started. Now that you're comfortable with the basic terms and concepts and you've read about an amazing investing success story, you're ready to really get into it. In this section, I'm answering the most common questions I get about saving for retirement to help you figure out where to start.

Where to Save for Retirement

You can start saving for retirement in an employer-sponsored retirement plan, your own independent retirement savings account (both of which have specific tax benefits), or in a non-retirement account (which does not have tax benefits but is still a means of saving). I explain the different retirement account types by name below.

401(k) – Employer sponsored: A 401(k) is a retirement plan that only an employer is allowed to offer. It allows employees to save and invest for retirement on a tax-deferred basis. This means you don't pay income tax right now on any amount you put into your 401(k). Eventually, in retirement, you'll pay income tax when you take disbursements from your funds at whatever your tax rate is at that time.

403(b), 457(b) – Employer sponsored: Similar to the 401(k), the 403(b) is specific to employees of public schools, certain tax-exempt organizations, and certain ministers, whereas the 457(b) is specific to governmental and certain nongovernmental employers and their employees.

Traditional IRA: A traditional IRA is an individual retirement account that allows you to make contributions with your pretax income up to a specified amount each year. Come retirement, you will have to pay taxes on any withdrawals you make on the account, just like with a 401(k). An IRA can be set up independently or offered by your employer.

Roth IRA: A Roth IRA is an individual retirement account that allows you to make contributions with your after-tax income up to a specified amount each year. Come retirement, your withdrawals will be tax free, including all interest you've earned. A Roth IRA can be set up independently or offered by your employer.

It's important to keep in mind that the eligible retirement age for the accounts listed above is 59½, and withdrawing funds earlier than this age can result in penalties and taxes. You can find out about the various retirement account contribution limits on the IRS website (http://IRS.gov).

Nonretirement accounts: Saving for retirement can happen outside of a "retirement savings" account as well. You can save for retirement in nonretirement accounts, which are basically brokerage accounts where you invest your after-tax money. While you won't enjoy any tax benefits like traditional retirement accounts, you'll still be saving money. Because you've paid taxes on your deposits, you'll only be required to pay taxes on your earned interest (capital gains) and there are no withdrawal penalties. So, while you don't benefit from the tax shelter, you also don't have to wait until age 59½ to take out your money.

Benefits and Drawbacks of Various Investment Plans

Employer Plans

When it comes to employer-sponsored accounts, some of them can be expensive and have hidden fees, and you will be limited to investing in only what is offered through your plan. That being said, investing in an employer's plan is a great way to take advantage of employer match programs if they are offered. Also, pretax investing plans typically have much higher contribution maximums than independently established retirement plans.

If you're not sure you'll stay with your employer for the long term, don't worry. Most people do not stay at their jobs for their entire career but still contribute to their employer's retirement plans. When you leave a job, you can roll over your employer's plan money into an independently established IRA, so you don't lose the money you've contributed. The nice thing about this is that you can then invest it more cost effectively (much lower fees) and with more transparency than your former employer's plan.

Taxes

Some investment plan contributions are made before taxes (like a 401(k), 457(b), 403(b), and traditional IRAs), which means that when you start to withdraw your money in retirement, you will be paying taxes at whatever your future tax rate is. Future tax rates are hard to predict, but they could possibly be higher than in the present day.

If you think your future tax bracket will be lower than what you currently pay, a traditional IRA is probably best for you – you'll benefit from a lower future tax rate. However, if you think your tax bracket will be higher than what it is now, a Roth IRA might be best since you would have already paid taxes on your contributions and therefore wouldn't have to pay income tax on your disbursements in retirement.

Many people have both types of IRA accounts (a traditional IRA and a Roth IRA), because ultimately they are able to save more by leveraging the benefits of these retirement plans over the long term. You just want to make sure you are aware of the qualification requirements put in place by the IRS.

By design, once you've reached age 59½, you are allowed to begin making withdrawals from your retirement accounts without penalties. Because retirement can last upwards of 20 years, you are not going to instantly withdraw all your money at that time. Your money actually still has more time to keep growing, and you should have an investment strategy in place that transitions to making your investments more conservative as you age to hedge against major losses that could occur from a market decline.

Concepts to Keep in Mind

Although we've gone over some general terms and concepts already, there are a few left that can be quite important when it comes to retirement accounts specifically. Keep these in mind as you plan for retirement:

Employer Matching

We've discussed this a bit already, but just to be clear, matching is a program that some employers offer to encourage you to invest in your retirement with them. When you contribute to their employer-sponsored retirement savings plan, they will match that amount (up to a certain limit) for free. Basically, they are giving you free money for investing in their plan. A match example could be a match of 100% for contributions up to 6% of your salary. This basically means that if you put up to 6% of your salary in your 401(k), your employer will match it in full. While you only pay 6% of your salary, your account is funded with 12%. If this type of program is offered by your employer, you definitely want to take advantage and get all of the free money they are offering you.

Retirement Plan Investment Options

When you put money into your employer-sponsored retirement savings accounts, you will have a few (although limited) options to invest in various stocks, funds, and target-date retirement funds. When you invest in your own independent IRA, however, you can make selections from the entire stock market – and there are no limitations to what you can purchase within your IRA contribution limit.

Early Withdrawals

If you decide to make early withdrawals from your account (i.e. before age 59½), you will be required to pay income tax on any pretax account distributions as well as an early-withdrawal penalty. As much as possible, don't withdraw any money from your retirement accounts. Leave that money there until you can take advantage of the benefits.

Retirement Plan Rollovers

I mentioned this earlier when speaking about changing jobs. A retirement plan rollover is an option to move your retirement savings from one employer to another if permitted by your new employer, or into your own IRA account.

If you are moving jobs, it's better to move your retirement savings into your own IRA account with a brokerage where you have access to the entire stock market and potentially much lower fees, as opposed to moving your money into your new employer's plan. Keep in mind that transferring the funds into a nonretirement investment account will be considered an early withdrawal and those distributions will be subject to income taxes (on pretax accounts) and an early-withdrawal penalty.

Investing for the long term is one of the keys to building real wealth, and your retirement savings falls under this category. If you haven't already, I highly recommended getting started as soon as you can with retirement savings. If you are already contributing to retirement savings, but are not maxing out your contributions, put a plan in place to make gradual increments over time until you get to the point where your contributions are fully maxed out each year.

Be sure to review the IRS website (http://IRS.gov) for qualification requirements and specifics on rules, restrictions, penalties, and exemptions.

How Much Do You Need?

The general take on retirement is that we need to have at least $1,000,000 in retirement savings. We hear it in the media, we see it on the news, we read it in finance books. But from your own personal perspective, do you know how much you really need to retire based on the things you want to do with your life? Let's talk through this a bit.

If you were to think about things on a monthly basis, how much money (in today's value) would you want to have available to spend each month of your retirement in order to feel comfortable? This monthly amount should include things like your living expenses, travel, fun, eating out. . .basically the cost of all the things you'd like to be able to afford for a full life when you are retired. Keep in mind that many retirees, even though they can afford to, never really retire 100% because they get bored and usually have part-time jobs or businesses. So when you think of that monthly amount, consider that you may have additional income coming in from a job or business.

Take that monthly amount and multiply by 12 so you know how much you need a year. So, for example, let's say you decide on $5000 a month, that's $60,000 a year that you'll need.

Now take that $60,000 and multiply it by 20 – this is about the average number of years that retirement lasts. That's $1.2 million. Now add 25% to get you the ballpark amount before taxes. So you'll need to save $1.5 million for retirement.

Once you know your retirement number, and you project what you are saving now into the future, are you on track? To determine this, find out how much you should be saving on an annual basis to ensure you meet your long-term retirement goal. Your calculation will, of course, need to factor in inflation. A good online retirement calculator can help you with that.

This exercise is not intended to scare you. Rather, it's meant to motivate you to create or adjust your long-term savings and investment strategy. If you haven't started saving, get started today. If you're not hitting that annual target, make a plan to get there.

The good news is that, thanks to compounding, you don't have to actually put the full amount away. If you contribute consistently to your retirement account and invest your contributions, your funds will compound over time and steadily grow. Look back to the section on compounding to see exactly how fast your money can grow. And remember, the only way you can get ahead is by getting started.

Take Action

Complete this exercise that outlines your plan to save for retirement:

1. Determine if your employer offers a 401(k) and if they have a match program. Make plans to contribute enough to get the full match, at the very minimum. If they offer a plan but do not have a match, it's still a good idea to contribute anyway to take advantage of the pretax benefits.
2. If they do not offer any sort of plan, determine which retirement savings option is best for you. Will it be a traditional IRA or a Roth IRA, or both (based on qualification guidelines)?
3. Determine how much you need to save for retirement. Figure out how much you'll need to contribute annually, starting now, to get to that amount.

HOW TO START INVESTING

Getting started with investing can seem daunting. There are so many options out there, and they all vary in terms of risk and return. However, now that you understand the basics of investing, you have the essential tools you'll need to start making those decisions.

You don't need to have a ton of money to start investing for retirement or for your other goals. All you need to do is set up an investing account with a brokerage firm or robo-advisor, decide how much you'd like to contribute, which types of investments you want to take on, and begin making small contributions over time.

While it's easy to get caught up with what everyone else is doing or saying when it comes to investing, it's important to keep in mind that your investment objectives and risk tolerance are personal and will very likely differ from that of the next person. Rather than going along with the popular opinion, make your own investment decisions.

To help you out, here are some guidelines or rules that every smart investor should know. Keep these in mind as you invest your money:

1. **Invest for the long term – five years or more.** As you decide how to invest your money, it's important to keep in mind that investing is for the long term. You should only be investing money that you won't need for at least five years or more – 10-plus years, if possible. Investing can be unpredictable, so you want to give your money time to grow and reap the rewards of compounding.

   The last thing you want to do is have to sell your investments during a market downturn. That being said, it's important to get rid of debt and create a solid emergency fund before starting to invest.
2. **Understand your fees.** Fees, also known as your investment expenses, can add up over the lifetime of your investment if you're not careful. I'm talking tens or even hundreds of thousands of dollars, depending on how much you have invested. It's important to understand the fees associated with your investments and shop around to ensure you are getting the best deal.

Fee types include:

- Brokerage commissions for buying and selling your investments
- Annual maintenance fees on your investment accounts
- Management fees for any investment advisors managing your portfolio

3. **Invest in funds instead of individual stocks.** Unless you have several hours each day to monitor your stocks, it's a better idea to invest in funds (i.e. mutual funds, index funds, or ETFs). These funds can help you create a well-diversified portfolio because they typically include a wide variety of stocks or bonds, which means you can avoid putting all your eggs in one basket.

   Keep in mind that you may have to pay additional fees for investing in a fund as opposed to an individual stock, especially if the fund is actively managed. It is also very important that you do your research to understand the composition and objectives of the funds you invest in. Personally, I'm a huge fan of index funds and ETFs due to their diversity and low cost.

4. **Determine your risk tolerance.** When you invest your money, you assume the risk of losing part of your investment, so it's a great idea to determine your risk tolerance. You want to ensure your tolerance level is in line with your investment objectives so you don't lose sleep every time there is a market dip.

   The longer you keep your money invested, the longer it has to grow and the longer it has to recover in the event of a market downturn or recession. You should never take on more risk than you can personally handle.

5. **Rebalance your portfolio.** To be sure you are staying on top of your investment objectives and timeline, set reminders to rebalance your portfolios every quarter or

at least every year. As the market changes and fluctuates, you'll want to ensure that your investments are balanced according to your long-term strategy.

With these guidelines in hand, you're well on your way to making smart investment decisions. However, you probably still have some questions and things to figure out. If that's the boat you're in, you might benefit from speaking with a financial advisor.

TIP

Educating yourself about different investment options and strategies before diving in can help you build confidence as an investor and minimize any investing fears you might have.

Do You Need a Financial Advisor?

Financial advisors are financial professionals who use their expertise to guide you on what to do with your money and how to meet your long-term goals. Many advisors have expertise in specific areas, such as investment management or retirement planning. As a result, they can help you determine your risk tolerance, time horizon, and best options for funds to invest in, and can manage your investments on your behalf. To offer this service, financial advisors typically complete specific training and hold professional certifications.

Advisors are especially useful if you're not confident in your investment knowledge or if you want someone to regularly monitor and adjust your investments for you. Basically, they're there to help you make smart choices with your money and build a portfolio that aligns with your financial goals and comfort level with risk.

However, having an advisor isn't necessary for everyone. You might not need a financial advisor if you're confident in your investment knowledge, have a simple financial situation and simple investments, prefer managing your investments yourself, or have access to reliable investment resources.

If you choose to work with an advisor, it is advisable to do your own financial research first so that you can have an informed conversation with them when you meet.

Some key considerations when selecting the right advisor include the following.

Fee type: Hiring a financial advisor can be expensive, so you'll want to understand exactly how their fees will work for your financial situation. Financial advisors use a fee model, and options are usually a flat fee, an hourly rate, or a percentage-based fee. Fees may differ by location and level of service. The key to remember is that the simpler your investment needs are, the less you'll have to pay.

Certifications and credentials: When you start working with a financial advisor, you're relying on them to guide you toward a stable financial future. It's important that your advisor has the appropriate certifications and qualifications, such as being a registered investment advisor. You should also seek out someone who acts as a fiduciary, meaning they prioritize your best interests. A reputable advisor will have met the standards set by the Financial Industry Regulatory Authority (FINRA).

Trust: When working with any advisor, trust is key. This is especially crucial when it comes to your finances because it can impact your future. As you seek out a financial advisor, be sure to have as many conversations as you need with them so you feel comfortable. It's also important that you conduct your own thorough research to ensure you have full confidence in their abilities. Look up reviews and seek referrals if possible.

Communication: If you're hiring an in-person financial advisor, be clear on how much access to them you'll have. Will they be available to answer your phone calls or respond to your emails quickly? How frequently will you be able to meet face to face? Make sure these expectations are set before you sign with them.

Investment philosophy: If you have specific beliefs about the impact of your investments, it's important to select a financial advisor who shares your values and comprehends your risk tolerance or level of risk aversion. For instance, if you prioritize ethical investing, ensure your advisor can select investments that align with your values. Ultimately, having a shared mission, values, and strategy with your advisor is crucial.

Whether you choose to work with a financial advisor or not, be sure to focus on empowering yourself to make informed investment decisions that align with your goals and preferences.

Take Action

1. Review all your investments and do your research to ensure you understand, at the very minimum, what you have invested in and the associated fees.
2. Additionally, ensure your investment portfolio is in line with your risk tolerance.
3. If necessary, schedule time with a brokerage firm or financial advisor to go over any questions or concerns you might have. Be sure to ask the following questions:
   - What is your fee type?
   - What certifications and credentials do you hold?
   - What is your communication style and frequency?
   - What is your investment philosophy?

MEET MABEL NUNEZ

Mabel is the founder and chief education officer at Girl$ on The Money (http://girlsonthemoney.com), a stock market investing education company for underrepresented individuals in the investing world.

She is passionate about helping women feel more confident around investing and empowering them to create wealth. Mabel teaches highly rated courses centered on stock market investing and is also the author of two best-selling books on the subject.

She holds a bachelor of science and an MBA in finance. However, most of what she's learned about the markets came from her personal experiences. She strongly believes investing is for everyone. No fancy degrees are necessary.

Mabel shares her experience being the first investor in her family and within her circle of friends.

Can you tell us about your journey as a first-generation stock market investor? What inspired you to start investing in the stock market?

> I was inspired to start investing immediately after taking a class in my senior year of college called "Investment Analysis," which was part of my major. The class was my first introduction to the stock market – ever! Before that, I knew no one in my circle of family, friends, or acquaintances who invested.
>
> I became fascinated with the idea of being a "part owner" of the biggest companies on the planet through stock investing. My professor did a fantastic job of explaining how investing works and how it is accessible to everyone, not just "the rich and famous." I would say that was what started my passion (or borderline obsession!) with the stock market.

What were some of the challenges you faced as a first-generation investor, and how did you overcome them?

> Since I didn't know anyone who invested, I was terrified of putting my money in an investment account and making decisions about what to buy. Although I was extremely excited about the topic and read and listened to everything I could get my hands on, I remained very fearful and hesitant.
>
> As God would have it, I eventually met someone at my first corporate job out of college who helped me let go of the fear. The person was a new hire at the company where I was working. They sat him right next to me and we soon got to talking. I learned that he was already an investor. During lunch hours, he

took the time to show me how investment accounts worked and how he made investment decisions.

After meeting a "real person" who invested and showed me the steps in "real time," I found the courage and confidence to (finally!) start my investing journey. I opened my first account that same week, and the rest is history!

What strategies did you use when selecting stocks to invest in? Did you focus on specific industries or sectors?

First and foremost, I focused on quality. My first introduction to the stock market was through individual stocks. (I wasn't introduced to index funds or ETFs until sometime later.)

From the beginning, I committed to investing my money in cream-of-the-crop businesses that were already successful and solid leaders within their respective industries. I had zero interest in penny stocks, startups, or anything speculative. I also had zero interest in gambling my money away on day trading.

From the beginning, I established a clear mission of building a portfolio composed of number-one leaders from various industries and sectors: the best of the best. It is a strategy I've continued to implement to this day and that has significantly contributed to my success as an investor. I also committed to being a long-term investor. (I still own the first stock I bought in 2008!)

Can you share a memorable investment success story and what you learned from it?

My most memorable success story has to be the first time I looked at my account and I noticed I had made thousands of dollars on one single stock in the tech sector (something I had held on to for a few years by then). I couldn't believe it and it just fueled my passion to continue investing! I still own this stock to this day, and it was one of the first investments that showed me the power of the stock market.

However, not all tech companies are created equal! There are many startups and "up-and-coming" companies in this space that sometimes crash and don't go anywhere. Be careful.

The key, in my opinion, is focusing on the businesses that have already proven themselves and have a strong track record of profitability and success, and also on those that are strong leaders in their respective industries and have a brand that is recognized all over the world.

Last time I checked, my return on investment on this stock was well over 500%. I don't check it often because it is a "no brainer" in my book. I know that the percentage constantly fluctuates because that's how the market works. I have no plans to sell. I am a proud shareholder and have been for a very long time.

Have you experienced any investment failures or setbacks? How did you handle them, and what lessons did you take away?

Yes! I invested in a particular stock in the retail industry. I quickly learned that what is "in style" and held in "high regard" today can quickly change tomorrow.

I first bought shares of the stock in 2013 and it was doing great until suddenly companies like Michael Kors, Kate Spade, and similar businesses within "affordable luxury" started to take away market share.

(Note: This was several years before Kate Spade got acquired and Michael Kors eventually went private. A lot of things have changed since then!)

The company also changed its business model and started to include discounted items, which used to be unheard of. The stock tumbled nearly 70% before I sold all my shares. I didn't sell everything at once because I was still holding on to hope for a while. However, it took longer than I expected for the company to find their way.

The company eventually changed its name and is now under a new business model and structure. The business seems to be doing great now. By the time that happened, I had already sold my shares.

All businesses struggle and go through rough patches. It didn't discourage me from investing as it was one of my best lessons despite the money lost.

How do you stay updated with market trends and economic developments that could impact your investments?

My favorite publication to stay in the know of stock market trends is the *Wall Street Journal*. I also consider them a credible source in a world where we are constantly faced with so much "fake news."

However, as a long-term investor, I don't let current events or macroeconomic factors impact my investment decisions. I like to quiet the noise as much as possible and get on with my life.

Based on your experience as a "first-generation" investor, what advice would you give other women who aspire to become first-generation investors?

Take action. I know that for me, that was key! Action breeds confidence and eliminates fear. Find someone you can trust who can teach you the steps of how legitimate investing works. You can also learn from reading investing books for beginners and listening to highly rated investing podcasts.

Don't fall into the trap of gambling your money away or following the "latest trends." That is a very risky approach that will lead you nowhere. Find an expert you can trust, start educating yourself, and start taking action.

Looking ahead, what are your long-term investment goals, and how do you plan to achieve them?

I want to continue growing my portfolio and achieving the financial milestones I have for myself, including buying property and early retirement.

One of the things investing allowed me to do was to have the freedom and flexibility to start a business with peace of mind. Thanks to investing, I left corporate America behind relatively young to pursue my own business (Girl$ on The Money). I will be forever grateful for that. It has been a true blessing and one of the things I am most proud of!

I plan to continue achieving my long-term investing goals by continuing the strategy that has worked for me all these years (investing in quality) and contributing more money to my investment accounts so that my money can continue working harder for me.

As a new mom, I also want to leave a legacy for my son. Not only financial, but I also want to teach him the skill of investing. It just takes one person in any family or generation to break the mold of lack of financial literacy, and that person was me!

PART III

The Necessary

Clever girls know. . .Financial success comes from strategic planning and good money management.

#CLEVERGIRLSKNOW

CHAPTER 6

Credit

Credit matters, but be mindful how you use it.

#CLEVERGIRLSKNOW

CREDIT 101

So far in these pages, we've looked at budgeting, debt, and saving – all important concepts when it comes to managing your money and building wealth. And through it all, we've spoken about paying off loans and credit card debt. But what we didn't cover – at least not yet – is how you can use your credit score to your advantage. When it comes to making big purchases like buying a home or financing a business, knowing and understanding your credit score and status is essential – especially if a certain score is required to qualify or if you intend to use some sort of financing.

So, since this concept can be so important for building wealth, let's start right at the beginning.

Your credit score or creditworthiness is used to determine your eligibility for pay-to-use services like a cell phone contract or your apartment rental and is also used to determine your interest rate and credit limits on your credit cards and loans. Some employers may also use your credit report as a determining factor when considering you for a job.

Your credit history is a record of how well you've paid your bills in the past and is used to determine your credit score. Financial institutions like banks and loan brokers report the amounts of money you owe, your track record for making payments, and any delinquencies on your accounts. Then various credit agencies use this information to determine your creditworthiness – or how risky it is to loan you money.

A credit report, on the other hand, is documentation of your credit history over time. This is basically a record of everything in your credit history. In the United States, there are three major credit bureaus: Equifax, Transunion, and Experian. Their main job is to collect your credit information from various sources, aggregate them into a report, assign you a credit score, and make this information available to your potential lenders.

Beginner Tips for Using Credit

Up until now, we've spoken about loans and credit cards as bad things. You don't want to go into debt and not be able to pay back what you owe. Not only do you spend more of your cash on interest payments, but you can negatively affect your ability to get good interest rates in the future if you're unable to make payments on time. With all that, though, there are ways to use credit to your advantage – and that all starts with maintaining a great credit score.

When was the last time you checked your credit? Is everything on your credit report documented accurately? Are all your bills being paid on time? Are you aware of any delinquencies? You should be able to answer all of these questions about your credit at any point in time. This way, you know your status before you apply for loans.

Knowing your credit score and what's in your credit history will also help you identify credit fraud or identity theft and resolve it if it happens to you – this is very important to catch early. Leaving issues like this over a long term will ruin your credit and can be a royal pain to fix.

Remember, you should use credit wisely and to your advantage, like for a home loan, getting a cell phone, renting an apartment, or acquiring business financing. These are all uses that will (most likely) benefit you now or in the future. Avoid racking up credit card debt, which, over the long term, costs too much and benefits you very little.

When it comes to your credit, the key to maintaining a great credit score is to never miss your bill payments. Avoid paying late or paying less than the minimum required. For credit cards, plan to pay your balance in full each month.

If you're intentional and objective about the way you use credit, you'll be sure to maintain a great credit score. This gives you a great advantage when it comes time to negotiate interest rates on all kinds of credit, including your credit cards and your mortgage. Keeping on top of your credit report and consistently checking to ensure the information is accurate will help you mitigate problems with identity theft or credit fraud. Now that you're clear on the basics, let's get into the details of credit scores.

CREDIT SCORES

Your credit score is a grading given to you by a credit bureau based on your credit history. It's used to help lenders determine or predict how well you will pay your bills in the future. Basically, if you have a high credit score, that shows you've been reliable with your payments in the past and that you're likely to be able to handle increased credit. If your score is low, it shows creditors that you haven't kept up with payments or you've misused credit, so you are more of a risk. Let's look more closely at the factors considered when determining your credit score.

Contributing Factors

The key contributing factors to your credit score include the following:

- Payment history: Your history of paying your credit bills on time. This history is a significant part of your credit score. Late payments, defaults, and debt in collections can have a negative impact.
- Credit utilization: This is the percentage of your available credit that you're using, also known as your debt to credit ratio. Keeping your credit utilization low (below 30% is recommended) can positively impact your credit score.
- Length of credit history: This is essentially the age of your accounts. A longer credit history demonstrates your ability to manage credit over time.
- Credit mix: These are the different types of credit accounts (e.g. credit cards, loans) you have. It shows that you can manage different types of credit responsibly.

- New credit: This is how many new lines of credit you have opened recently. Opening multiple new lines of credit within a short period of time may indicate to lenders that you have money troubles and may lower your credit score temporarily.
- Credit inquiries: When a lender checks your credit report based on a loan or credit application, it can trigger a hard inquiry. This can lower your credit score temporarily. Keep in mind that soft inquiries (like you checking your own credit) do not impact your score.

Now, when it comes to determining your score, most people are under the impression that there is just one number that is always used. This is the number that many people worry about, focus on, and are continuously trying to improve. But did you know there are different credit scoring methods used by various credit bureaus and lenders?

Let's talk about the two most commonly used credit scoring methods.

The FICO Score

The FICO scoring method is most popular and was created by a company called, you guessed it, FICO (Fair Isaac Corporation). One interesting fact to know is that your FICO Score may vary from lender to lender and across the three major credit bureaus because there are multiple versions of the FICO Score. These multiple versions are due to updates to the FICO scoring model over time and industry-specific FICO Scores.

FICO Scoring Model Updates

According to the myfico.com website, evolving credit scoring models are described as follows:

> Think of how people use different versions of computer operating systems or have older or newer generations of

> smart phones. They all share the same base functionality, but the latest versions also have unique updated features to meet evolving user needs. The same goes for FICO® Scores. The various FICO® Score versions all have a similar underlying foundation, and all versions effectively identify higher risk people from lower risk people. Every time the FICO Score algorithm is updated it incorporates unique features, leverages new risk prediction technology, and reflects more recent consumer credit behaviors. The end result is a more predictive score that helps lenders make more informed lending decisions, which ultimately makes the credit process easier, faster, and fairer.

Note: The base FICO Score ranges from 300 to 850, with a higher score indicating better credit.

Industry-Specific FICO Scores

Additionally, industry-specific FICO Scores are tailored FICO Score versions designed for specific credit products like mortgages, auto loans, or credit cards. While they share the foundational elements of the base FICO Score versions, they are customized to reflect industry-specific risk behaviors. Keep in mind that industry-specific scores may utilize a wider FICO Score scale ranging from 250 to 900. According to FICO, this range provides lenders with a more refined credit risk assessment tailored to the type of credit the consumer is seeking.[1]

How Your FICO Score Is Determined

In order to create your score, FICO assesses credit information that's kept on file about you by the three major credit bureaus (Experian, Equifax, and Transunion). This information is reported to the credit bureaus by various creditors, some of whom may be

[1]https://www.myfico.com/credit-education/credit-scores/fico-score-versions

using a different FICO Score model or industry-specific model. As result, you may have a different FICO score from each of the credit bureaus based on how they track your score. While lenders have a choice of credit scores to use when evaluating you for credit, the FICO scoring model is the most popular option.

Factors used to calculate your FICO scores include payment history, debt owed, length of credit history, new credit, and your credit mix.[2] All of these factors are considered in other credit score models as well, though, so if you have a good FICO score, you can safely assume your other credit scores will follow suit.

VantageScore

VantageScore is FICO's main competitor. This credit scoring method was created jointly by Equifax, Transunion, and Experian in 2006 with the goal of creating a more consistent credit scoring method. It uses credit information from all three bureaus, but your actual VantageScore may vary across bureaus due to the date your score was pulled and when creditors report on your credit (it can vary for each bureau).

Factors used to calculate your VantageScore include payment history, credit utilization, type of account and age, total balance, new credit, and available credit.[3] The VantageScore also ignores paid collection accounts and all of your paid or unpaid medical debt in collections, regardless of the amount or the age of the debt.[4]

Although FICO is the most well-known, 8 of the top 10 bank lenders and 30 of the top 50 bank lenders use the VantageScore credit scores. In fact, over a period of 12 months between January and December 2023, more than 3,400 companies used 27 billion

---

[2]https://www.myfico.com/credit-education/whats-in-your-credit-score

[3]https://www.experian.com/blogs/ask-experian/what-is-a-vantagescore-credit-score/

[4]https://www.experian.com/blogs/ask-experian/the-difference-between-vantage-scores-and-fico-scores

VantageScore credit scores to make lending decisions.[5] The current VantageScore range, similar to the base FICO Score range, is 300–850.

■ ■ ■

While there are many different credit models that exist out there, these two are the most popular ones. When applying for credit, you can ask your lender what credit score or scores they will be basing their decision upon and find out for yourself what your score is. This way, you'll know in advance if you're likely to be approved and what kind of rate you can expect.

With all that said, it's a good idea to monitor your credit report and keep on top of the information being reported. The more diligent you are with this, the better you will be at catching inaccuracies and protecting yourself from credit fraud.

Checking Your Credit Report

A lot of people are not aware of this, but in the United States, you are entitled to a free credit report from each of the three credit bureaus (Experian, Equifax, and Transunion) once every year. You can order these free reports online at annualcreditreport.com.

Improving Your Credit Score

According to myfico.com, a "good" credit score is between 670 and 739, while a credit score between 740 and 799 is considered "very good."[6]

This means that you'll more than likely be approved for a loan at the best possible interest rate. So, ideally, your goal should be to get as close to these ranges as possible. In addition to qualifying for better interest rates, improving your credit score makes you more attractive to lenders, landlords, and even some employers.

---

[5]https://www.vantagescore.com/faq/who-uses-vantagescore-models/

[6]https://www.myfico.com/credit-education/credit-scores

In order to improve your credit score, you need to make sure you know what is currently on your credit report, pay all your bills and loans on time, and reduce your overall debt-to-credit ratio by paying down debt. Regardless of your credit card limits, you want to keep your credit card balances to the minimum and pay them off in full each month.

Rebuilding or Maintaining Your Credit

Again, according to myfico.com, a score of 580 or lower is considered "poor credit" while a score between 580 and 669 is considered "fair."[7] If your credit score falls anywhere in this area and you need to secure some sort of financing in the near future (e.g. for a house or a car), you should be concerned about improving your credit score.

As I've mentioned, having good credit means you can get the best available interest rates when it comes to credit and financing. It also lets landlords and employers know how you handle bill payments and therefore demonstrates how responsible you are with money. Clearly, having good credit is important, so let's look at a few ways you can work to improve your rating:

- **Get a copy of your current credit report from all three credit bureaus.** First things first, you want to know where you currently stand with your credit. You need to understand what has been reported about you, how much you owe, your different account types, and any late payments or delinquencies that have been recorded. Once you understand what has been reported, you can dispute any inconsistencies and have those issues removed from your record.
- **Pay your bills on time, and catch up on your payments.** Paying your bills on time proves your creditworthiness to

[7]https://www.myfico.com/credit-education/credit-scores

lenders and has a huge impact on your credit score. If you are behind on any payments, you need to get caught up as soon as you can. Call your creditors, create payment plans, and set up new payment dates.

Set reminders for yourself for all your bills to make sure you don't forget to make any payments in the future.

TIP

Build all your recurring payments along with their due dates into your budget. You should also consider automating your payments.

- **Pay down your debt.** Your overall debt load, as well as your percentage of credit utilization, affects your credit score. Let's say you have a credit card with a limit of $1,000 and you owe $950 on it; your utilization is 95%. This high utilization can count against you because creditors use it as a gauge to see how likely you are to pay back what you owe.

  A high utilization makes you less attractive to a creditor, so reducing your debt load can increase your score immensely. Keep in mind the goal of paying down your debt shouldn't just be for a good credit rating. By paying down debt, you save yourself tons of money in interest payments that you can then put toward long-term savings and investing.
- **Avoid too many new credit applications over a short period of time.** Applying to and opening too many new lines of credit over a short period of time can have a negative impact on your credit. When you apply for new credit, lenders will typically run a hard inquiry on your credit report, which can lower your score slightly for a short period of time.

Additionally, multiple credit applications in a short timeframe might make lenders think you have money troubles and raise concerns about your ability to pay back the debt. So space out your credit applications (it's a good idea to wait six months between applications), and only apply for new lines of credit when you really need to. This will show lenders you are responsible with credit.

- **Don't close your old credit card accounts.** Your credit card accounts make up a vital part of your credit report, specifically your credit history. If you have accounts that show you've been paying your bills on time consistently, keep them as part of your credit history.

  If they are accounts you have paid off, keep them open and make the occasional small purchase on them and then pay it off in full each month. If they are accounts you are actively paying off, over time those on-time payments will positively impact your overall credit score and reduce your credit utilization. If you do decide to close your account for a specific reason, be sure to pay down any other credit card balances you have first to avoid an increase in your overall credit utilization rate. This is because once you close a credit card account, it reduces your overall available credit across all your lines of credit, which in turn can impact your debt-to-credit ratio.
- **Be smart about your finances.** Pay off and avoid debt, build an emergency fund, save for retirement, check your credit frequently – these are all things you should be doing over the long term. Establishing good financial habits ensures you avoid scenarios that will impact your credit.

  When you take care of your finances, your credit score should improve. As you automate your bill payments and include them in your budget, you ensure all your accounts are up to date. As you pay down your debt, your credit utilization decreases. These two factors, along with the positive credit history you'll be building, will ensure your credit score continues to increase, leaving you with much better opportunities for accessing credit in the future. While maintaining a good credit score is important, you'll want to pay extra attention to this if you intend to buy a house or apply for a business loan in the near future.

Are Credit Repair Companies a Good Idea?

I get asked so often if hiring a credit repair company is a good idea. In my opinion, you don't need a credit repair company to build or repair your credit. You can do it yourself by taking specific actions as outlined in this chapter; check your credit and dispute any errors, pay your bills on time, pay down debt to bring down your credit utilization, avoid too many new credit applications, don't close out all your lines of credit, and be smart about how you spend on credit.

It's also important to be patient because it can take time for you to see the fruit of your efforts reflected on your credit report.

If, however, you do decide to work with a credit repair company, keep in mind there is usually a fee involved, so make sure you understand exactly what you're paying for. It's also incredibly important to do your homework.

Unfortunately, there are a lot of scams out there in the credit repair space, so you need to make sure you are dealing with a reputable company. Be wary of anyone promising you overnight results.

Is Freezing Your Credit a Good Idea?

Freezing your credit is essentially like putting a lock on your financial information. It stops people from opening new accounts or loans in your name without your permission and in turn helps prevent identity theft.

By freezing your credit, you gain better control over who can access your credit report, reducing the risk of fraudulent activities and unauthorized inquiries. This added layer of security provides peace of mind, especially for those who have experienced identity theft in the past or are concerned about the security of their personal information.

As a victim of identity theft and credit fraud myself, I am personally a fan of freezing my credit, especially after my identity was stolen and a transaction worth thousands of dollars was made in my name. It's better to be proactive than reactive when it comes to protecting your finances. Keep in mind that freezing your credit doesn't impact your credit score or your ability to use your existing credit accounts.

You can freeze your credit with each of the three major credit bureaus – Equifax, Transunion, and Experian – on their websites:

- Equifax: www.equifax.com/personal/credit-report-services/credit-freeze/
- TransUnion: www.transunion.com/credit-freeze
- Experian: www.experian.com/freeze

It's important to note that you'll need to contact each bureau individually to freeze your credit.

BUSTING CREDIT MYTHS

Yup, there are quite a number of myths out there that certainly have an impact on credit confidence and proper decision-making around the use of credit. It's time to dispel them.

Myth 1: Paying your cell phone bill builds your credit score.

Unfortunately, paying your phone bill does not affect your credit score. However, if you pay your bill late and become delinquent, it will have a negative impact on your credit score. So if your focus is on building your credit, use a credit card responsibly and pay your balance in full each month. Also, be sure to stay current with your payments on other loans or outstanding debts you might have.

Myth 2: Carrying a credit card balance is good for your credit.

Wrong! Carrying a balance on your credit card isn't a great idea. Not only will you owe money (and therefore pay interest), but you'll increase your credit utilization, which can negatively impact your credit score. You should strive to pay your credit card bill in full and on time every month to build and protect your credit score.

Myth 3: Closing unused credit cards is good for your credit.

No, closing your credit card accounts isn't better for your credit than keeping them open. On the contrary, the average age of your accounts is a significant factor in your credit score, so keeping your oldest cards open will typically help your score.

At a minimum, you can plan to make small transactions every few months that you pay off in full at the end of the billing cycle to keep your unused credit card active. However, if you struggle with overspending and lack the discipline to stay out of credit card debt, closing your accounts might be better for you personally. Just keep in mind that it may impact your credit score.

Myth 4: You only have one credit score.

Based on the previous section, you now know that you have more than one credit score and that the different credit bureaus all have different methods of calculating those scores. If you're concerned, you can always get your score from each bureau to see how they compare.

Myth 5: Checking your credit report will not reduce your credit score.

If you are applying for loans or lines of credit, you are most likely getting "hard" inquiries against your credit report. A hard inquiry for credit applications or credit checks can cause a temporary dip in your score, but "soft" inquiries, such as checking your credit score through credit monitoring tools, will not impact it. So it's important to know the difference. Many lenders now offer qualification checks using "soft" inquiries. This approach allows you to determine if you are eligible for a loan before you submit an actual application.

Keep that in mind that as you build your credit, you want to avoid too many hard inquiries. If you want to keep a close eye on it, you're better off subscribing to a monitoring service. Both Experian and Transunion offer a level of credit monitoring services for free through their websites (Experian: www.experian.com/credit/credit-monitoring; Transunion: www.transunion.com/product/trueidentity-free-identity-protection).

Once you sign up you will get alerted to any changes to your credit. Additionally, many banks and credit card companies also offer credit monitoring and tracking services for free, so you can check with your bank or credit card company as well.

Myth 6: A bad credit score cannot be rebuilt.

A lot of people believe that when your score is low, there's no chance you'll ever improve it. That's simply not true. Your credit can be rebuilt over time if you focus on developing good habits and working through the issues on your credit report. Things like paying your bills on time and in full, coming to agreements with collection agencies for delinquent accounts, or getting credit counseling or coaching are options you have that will help you rebuild your credit.

When it comes to credit, it's all about having the right information and taking the proper steps to ensure you maintain your credit score for when you need it.

COMPROMISED INFORMATION

Up to this point, you've worked hard to sort out your finances. You've organized your files, created and followed a budget, started saving for your financial goals, and begun work to improve your credit score. You've put in so much time and effort to ensure you're financially safe, and you don't want anything to come in and destroy that.

In this day and age, though, identity theft and compromised information are all too common. It seems like every few months there is a new report about a security breach that has the potential to leave masses of people susceptible to identity theft and credit fraud.

As I mentioned earlier, I have been a victim of both – and I can tell you from experience that it's a nightmare to deal with. Luckily for me, I was able to resolve these situations with minimal impact because I figured it out early enough and got my money back. However, for many, that isn't the case; these problems can take months and sometimes years to rectify.

Protecting yourself from identity theft and credit fraud can be incredibly important to your long-term success. Here are some key things you need to do to minimize the impact and protect yourself:

- **Stay on top of checking your credit.** You want to make sure everything on your credit report is as expected and all the reported activity is your own. You are entitled to a free report from all three credit bureaus each year via annualcreditreport.com – or you can choose to pay for one. The bottom line is that you need to check your credit to make sure nothing strange is going on there.
- **Get credit monitoring in place or consider a credit freeze.** If you find a breach has occurred, know that it could take months or years for you to be affected. Usually, when a company has been impacted by a security breach,

they typically offer free credit monitoring of some sort for a period of time. If you're in this boat, I highly recommend you take advantage of it. Also, consider a credit freeze as well, which will restrict access to your credit report and reduce the chances that someone will access unauthorized lines of credit in your name.

If nothing has happened yet, but you're worried it could, there are several subscription options for credit monitoring.

- **Change any passwords and PINs.** For your general security, it's a good idea to regularly change your passwords and PINs, especially on accounts that have your financial information associated with them. If a breach of your information does occur, change those passwords and PINs immediately. Sometimes it's hard to determine exactly what information was breached, so it's better to take all precautions and remain proactive.

Something's Fishy – Now What?

If you find out that you've been the victim of identity theft or credit fraud, you'll want to take action to rectify the situation as quickly as possible:

1. Start by pulling a copy of your credit report to determine what damage might have been done. Take some time out to review your bank and credit card statements for any discrepancies in case the transactions have not yet been reported on your credit profile.
2. Alert credit bureaus to the situation and place a fraud alert or freeze on your reports to prevent any additional damage.
3. Contact your creditors or service providers to report the situation and dispute any fraudulent claims made in your name.

4. File a police report and get a copy of this report to share with credit bureaus and creditors as part of your case file.
5. If you think your Social Security number has been compromised, contact the Social Security Administration (ssa.gov) to file a report.
6. Be sure to contact the post office as well, in the event that an unauthorized change of address has been filed in your name.

Take Action

To make sure you are on top of your credit, here are a few things you can do:

1. Pull your credit reports and review them in detail. You can get a free copy of your report from all three credit bureaus at annualcreditreport.com.
2. Put monitoring on your credit so you are aware of any changes that occur, including any fraudulent activity or attempts.
3. If you are unsure whether your financial information has been compromised, follow the steps in this section on what to do as soon as possible. Otherwise, maintain a close watch on your credit reports and accounts so you can catch a breach as soon as possible.

MEET ROSEMARY A.B.

Rosemary is a "Zennial" first-generation immigrant on a journey of building first-generation wealth. She is also part of the Clever Girl Finance community.

Rosemary shares how she educated herself about credit and built her own good credit standing as she worked on paying down her debt.

Can you tell us about the early stages of your journey as a first-generation immigrant building first-generation wealth?

My journey started in college. I attended a small private liberal arts college in Georgia where I received an academic scholarship that covered tuition but did not cover room and board. So I took out about $10,000 in student loans to live on campus, which was required of students from freshman to junior year. After my first year, I transferred to a public university in North Carolina, primarily because my parents lived there. This was one of the best things I did because I was fortunate to receive needs-based grants that covered the entire cost of my college attendance (including my tuition, room, and board, as well as my books) for the three years I had left. This move helped me avoid taking on more student loan debt, and as a result I was able to save a large portion of my tuition refund checks and put it toward financing a car.

I also had several internships in college but my experience at one was crucial to my wealth-building journey. While there, I had a conversation with a team member who was in his late 20s or early 30s. He encouraged me to open a Roth IRA while I was young. He didn't share too much about the mechanics of Roth IRAs, but I got the impression that it was a good idea, so I kept that in mind.

I did, however, manage to get myself into credit card debt. I had one credit card with a $1,500 limit, which I typically paid off each month. That was until Beyoncé went on tour and I put the concert tickets on my card. Before I knew it, my credit card utilization was at about 90% and I was only able to make the minimum payments. This made me incredibly uncomfortable because it took me back to my childhood memories of my mom paying off her JCPenney store credit card. I knew credit card debt was bad.

All said and done, I graduated with about $22,000 of debt – $10,000 in federal student loans, $10,000 in an auto loan, and $2000 in credit card debt. As soon as I got a job, I started investing in my employer's 401(k) plan and at the same time paying down my debt and establishing an emergency fund. With each salary increase, I increased my 401(k) contributions. I also saved 90% of my bonuses at work, which went straight to my emergency fund. About a year later, I remembered the conversation I had with the teammate at my internship about opening a Roth IRA, so I opened an account with a robo-advisor and made monthly contributions.

As time went by, life happened. I paid off my car but then had to drain my emergency fund, and I took on another $10,000 of debt to get a new car. I was, however, able to replenish my emergency fund and I maxed out my Roth IRA for the first time shortly afterward. A few years later I also maxed out my 401(k) for the first time and opened a taxable brokerage account. Additionally, the 2020 COVID-19 federal student loan moratorium[8] that automatically paused student loan payments and set interest rates to 0% worked in my favor because I continued to make payments and I was able to pay down my loan faster due to the 0% interest rate.

I eventually sold my car when I moved to a walkable city, which paid off the loan and gave me a $10,000 windfall due to positive equity. This is when

[8]https://studentaid.gov/announcements-events/covid-19

I officially became debt free, and at the time I also had a little over $100,000 invested across my 401(k), Roth IRA, HSA, and taxable brokerage accounts.

What motivated you to focus on educating yourself about credit and improving your credit standing?

Luckily, I've always had good credit from when I needed it after graduation. A main contributor is that I made sure I paid my credit card bill on time each month while I was in college even when I was only making minimum payments. My mother had also made me an authorized user on her credit cards when I was a teenager, which gave me a credit history and thankfully it had nothing but positive effects on my credit score.

That said, educating myself about how credit worked became important when I learned how easy you have it when you have good credit, and my journey to learning about credit actually started with the *Clever Girls Know Podcast*! I played the episodes while running errands or doing chores. Listening to various episodes piqued my interest to research my credit report and my credit score across the different credit bureaus and to learn more about the factors that played into my score. Because I have maintained my credit score over time, I have never had to pay a deposit for electricity or had to pay a housing deposit.

What were some of the challenges you faced while paying down your debt, and how did you overcome them?

The challenges I experienced were mostly superficial ones. Paying down debt comes at an opportunity cost; putting extra money to pay down debt means less money goes to leisure. There were definitely times when I experienced FOMO, but ultimately I didn't deprive myself of the small pleasures I enjoyed while getting out of debt. I think this helped keep me motivated as I paid down my debt.

How are you maintaining your credit today?

I always make on-time payments to my credit card because payment history impacts your credit score the most and I aim to pay off my balance each month. I also make on-time payments on healthcare bills (no matter how small) to avoid them going to collections and negatively impacting my credit score.

What advice would you give to others who are also looking to build wealth and improve their credit standing?

- **Create a debt payoff plan and avoid taking on debt if possible.** The right payoff plan is the one that works for you. This could be paying off debt with the highest balance or lowest balance. Whatever it is, make sure you're not accumulating more debt through your actions (e.g. spending more than you have or continuing to add on to your existing credit card balance).
- **Start small and build up your portfolio over time when it comes to investing.** Use online estimators to determine how much you need to save over time and take advantage of your employer's retirement savings plan if you have access to one.
- **Use your credit card like a debit card,** meaning only charge an expense to your credit card that you can pay off each month, and be sure to make payments on time. I use a credit card that has great rewards programs like presale concert tickets, free meal/grocery delivery membership, and access to travel perks, but I build my spending into my monthly budget.

CHAPTER 7
Protecting Yourself

Insurance is the backup to your backup.

#CLEVERGIRLSKNOW

CREATING A BACKUP PLAN WITH THE RIGHT INSURANCE

Although most people don't like thinking about it, bad things can and do happen in life. Your basement could flood, or you could become ill or disabled. What about a car accident or, God forbid, a death in your family? They aren't pleasant to think about, but the truth is, you need to ensure you protect yourself against these possibilities.

Having the right insurance can potentially save you a ton of money in the event of an emergency or unplanned life occurrence. It means you can protect yourself without having to impact your financial plans or offset your goal timelines. On the flipside, not having adequate insurance can derail your financial goals, and you definitely don't want that!

I've been in a few situations where having the right kind of insurance made all the difference. When I was pregnant with my twins, my pregnancy turned out to be high risk, which meant several doctors' visits, lots of testing, and even a few hospital admissions – all very expensive medical care. In addition, I had to have an emergency C-section and stay in the hospital for an extended period. After all was said and done, my medical bills just for that pregnancy came out to almost $45,000. Luckily, having the right insurance made all the difference, and I only had to pay $5,000 out of pocket.

Another time, I was rear-ended in my car. The repairs and hospital bill came to $8,000 in all. Again, having the right kind of insurance made all the difference. I simply paid my $500 deductible. Even though the accident meant a huge repair cost, a rental car, and a hospital visit, my financial plans remained intact thanks to the insurance I had.

Although insurance can often feel like an unnecessary cost – especially if you've never had to use it – you'll find that over the course of your life, you'll be thankful that you had it, at least once. But what's challenging about insurance is knowing exactly what you need and what will be covered. In this section, I'll outline several types of insurance you should consider getting.

Health Insurance

In the United States, the cost of healthcare is high, so having health insurance is necessary. Seeing a doctor can run you anywhere from $100 to $300 out of pocket for an initial consultation – or more if you need a procedure done or require serious medical attention.

According to the Peterson-KFF Health System Tracker (healthsystemtracker.org), at the time of this writing, depending on where you are located, the costs associated with pregnancy, childbirth, and postpartum care average $4,768 for a regular delivery to upward of $26,280 or more for a C-section before any insurance coverage. With insurance coverage, the average out-of-pocket expense for a regular delivery is $2,655 and for a C-section it's $3,214.[1] Having health insurance allows you to get the right care when you need it and reduce the financial burden of having to pay completely out of pocket because instead you'll only have to pay a co-pay.

Many employers offer health insurance plans to employees. If this is available to you, look into it and take advantage if it makes financial sense. If nothing is offered where you work, there are plenty of private plans that offer great coverage. The federal government website (https://finder.healthcare.gov/) can help you find private healthcare options for various budgets and needs.

Auto Insurance

First of all, not having auto insurance in the United States is illegal and punishable by law. If you own a car, you must have auto insurance. However, you can get coverage above and beyond the

[1]https://www.healthsystemtracker.org/brief/health-costs-associated-with-pregnancy-childbirth-and-postpartum-care/

legal minimums if you want extra coverage. Not only does auto insurance cover the cost of repairs incurred from a car accident after you meet the deductible requirements, but it also covers hospital bills you or the other driver might incur, rental cars if yours will be out of commission, and protection against legal action.

If you currently pay for the legal minimum in auto insurance, look into additional coverage. You might find the benefits offered are advantageous to your particular situation.

Renter's Insurance

If you are renting your home, you are not responsible for the actual building or major repairs. However, you may want to consider getting renter's insurance to cover the valuables you keep at home in the event that they ever get damaged by flooding, fire, or another disaster – or in the event that your home is broken into. This type of insurance would cover electronics and other valuables and is very affordable.

Homeowner's Insurance

If you own a home, insurance is essential. Imagine if you had to rebuild your house or replace everything you have in your home out of pocket. That could be financially devastating! Plus, if you've financed your home with a mortgage, insurance on your home was likely required in order to close. This type of insurance protects your home against damages to the house itself and to possessions within the home in the case of a theft or damage from a natural disaster. If you live in an area prone to flooding or tornados, you can add on specific natural disaster insurance to your insurance coverage to further protect your home.

Insuring Your Home-Based Business or Home Office

If you have a home-based business or a home office and you already have homeowner's insurance, be sure that your policy covers your business and all the equipment in your home office.

You can also get independent business or office insurance that will provide you with coverage as well. This way, in the event of damage or a burglary, your business is still protected.

Protecting Your Home Against Burglary

No one ever wants it to happen to them, but burglaries and break-ins do occur. In fact, in the United States there are about 1.7 million of them every year. Clearly, it's a good idea to protect your home from these situations. Consider getting an alarm system installed (you may qualify for discounts on your insurance policy if you have one), make sure there is good lighting at your entryway, and install strong locks or deadbolts on your doors.

In addition, be sure to check all your windows frequently to make sure they are locked when you are not home or you are sleeping. Also consider buying a safe to store things like important documents and jewelry in your home – bonus points if it's fireproof and waterproof!

Life Insurance

Although it's not necessary for everyone, life insurance is something to consider if you have dependents. For example, if your income is essential to your family's welfare, or if you have children or other major financial commitments, you will benefit from having life insurance. The main purpose of life insurance is to provide a lump-sum payment to your dependents in the event of your death. Life insurance is often thought to be quite complicated because of the different types you can buy and the varying amounts of coverage. In reality, what you need might be quite simple.

Term Life Insurance

You pay an annual premium according to the amount of coverage you want. In the event of your death, your beneficiaries are paid a lump sum. Usually, you'd take your annual income and multiply it by the number of years you want your family to be covered.

Cash Value Insurance (Universal or Whole Life)

This is a combination of your standard life insurance and some sort of cash value feature. With this type of insurance, the longer you pay, the more money your beneficiaries receive. You can also leverage your built-up cash value. While this type of life insurance sounds attractive, it is also more expensive, so you'll want to keep that in mind.

Regardless of what type of life insurance you choose, you want to make sure you fully understand what is associated with each, how much coverage the premium provides, and if there are any conditions or requirements that must be met before you can benefit.

Long-Term Disability Insurance

This insurance covers you by replacing your income in the event that you are unable to work due to a permanent or temporary disability. Whether or not you have dependents, if you have monthly living expenses, then you definitely want to look into getting disability insurance.

If you determine this is right for you, look into the requirements for approval, which disabilities are covered, and how much you will benefit for the premium you pay. Not all insurance is equal.

Personal Article Insurance

Got an expensive engagement ring or wedding ring set? A one-of-a-kind watch? A laptop you take with you everywhere? If you have any personal items that are of value that you often have with you outside of your home, consider insuring them through a personal articles policy. This type of insurance covers theft, damage, and loss of expensive items.

Pet Insurance

If you're a pet person, pet insurance can be beneficial. Medical care for your pets can be incredibly expensive if they are injured or diagnosed with an illness. Because they are a part of your family, you'll want to be sure you can give them the best care possible. Keep in mind that as your pet gets older, the more medical attention they might need. Having this type of insurance will save you from going broke to take care of your family pet.

With all of that said, remember that not all insurance is necessary. It can sound really nice to have coverage for any and all possibilities, but the reality is that insurance can turn out to be pretty pricey. You'll want to make sure that whatever additional insurance coverage you get fits into your budget and makes sense for your life situation. You also want to be sure that the potential payout from an insurance policy far outweighs the cost you'll be paying to have the coverage over time.

TIP

One great way to find the best insurance rates is to shop around and compare quotes from different insurance companies. See what each company offers in terms of coverage, deductibles, and any discounts they might have. It's all about getting the best value for your insurance premiums.

Take Action

Use the following tips to assess the insurance you currently have and still need:

1. Review your various insurance policies to determine what's covered and if there are any gaps you want to fill.

2. Make some time to inquire about extra coverage, new policies, and even new providers.
3. Make note of future insurance needs you might have based on upcoming life changes.

Always be prepared.

#CLEVERGIRLSKNOW

RECESSION-PROOFING YOUR FINANCES

Have you ever considered what could happen if you lost your job? What if you couldn't find a new one for a while? Or what if you had to take a pay cut for an extended period of time? Well, that's what often happens in a bad economy. In fact, recessions are fairly common and can have huge impacts on your financial health.

Economies are cyclical, which means they go through periods of expansion and growth that can go on for several years, followed by periods of decline like recessions and depressions. This happens because when there is growth, there is also overproduction and overconsumption, so after a while, it becomes hard to keep up with and maintain that momentum.

During a recession, there is typically a decline in industrial and trade activity, and this can severely impact your personal finances. For instance, production of goods decreases and services become limited because there is less demand. As these changes take place, there are typically increased layoffs, more unemployment, drops in real estate value, and declines in investment values. This means you could potentially lose some value in your retirement fund and/or your home, and you could even face unemployment.

However, regardless of whether or not there is a recession going on, life goes on and bills need to be paid. So what do you do? Well, if you aren't prepared, you could end up going into a lot of debt. But that's what we're here to avoid. Rather than waiting to see what happens in a recession, a better plan is to prepare yourself and your finances. Establish a plan for yourself where, in the event of a bad economy, the impact on your personal finances and financial goals is minimal.

Here are five important things you need to be doing now so a future recession is not financially devastating:

1. **Bulk up your emergency savings.** I've mentioned your emergency savings several times throughout this book. While you know you should plan to have three to six

months' worth of funds in your account, when talk of a recession is coming, it's a great idea to boost that amount to about 12 months' worth of funds. This will give you ample time to find a new job, since jobs can be harder to come by in an economy experiencing a recession.

2. **Pay off debt.** When a recession hits, the last thing you want to do is worry about having to pay off debt, especially if you might lose your job. So start working to pay down your debt. Not only will you save money in interest payments but you'll also be able to put your extra funds toward bulking up your emergency savings and other financial goals.
3. **Diversify your investments.** In the investing chapter, you learned all about the different types of investments and building an investment portfolio. The most important lesson here is not to put all your eggs in one basket. It's important to have a diversified investment portfolio so that your money isn't all tied up in one stock or one property.

   You want to make sure your investments are spread across multiple industries and areas, so that if one industry or area experiences a decline, it doesn't completely sink your entire portfolio. For example, if you are invested in the stock market, you can spread your investments across multiple sectors such as consumer goods, healthcare, and technology. Mutual funds, index funds, and exchange-traded funds are a great way to diversify. You can also have a combination of investments in the stock market, real estate, and small businesses.

   If you have a clear plan for your investments that you adjust based on your objectives, and you plan to stay in it for the long term, your investments are very likely to weather a bad economy and come out on top. Talk to a financial advisor if you are confused or feeling stuck when it comes to creating a diversified portfolio.
4. **Learn how to budget and live within your means.** Living within your means is the key to building wealth. Rather

than spending on things you really can't afford, learn to follow a budget that is designed around your income. Your budget will help you track your expenses in comparison to what you earn and will highlight areas you can cut back on.

Some signs that you are living above your means include things like spending money on nonessentials, when you don't yet have an emergency fund in place, impulse purchases causing you to carry a credit card balance, and not saving or investing any of your income because of your nonessential and impulse spending. Living within your means allows you to become debt-free sooner and can even improve your credit score. As a result, you'll have fewer money worries, build savings faster, and your financial confidence will be boosted.

Your ultimate goal should be to widen the gap between your income and expenses as much as you can, because the money you have left over is money you can use toward the things that really matter – your savings and investment goals.

5. **Create multiple income streams.** It's popularly said that the average millionaire has seven different sources of income – and for good reason. Creating multiple streams of income not only ensures that you increase how much you earn overall but also acts as a buffer in case one of those streams fails. If there's something you are passionate about doing or something you do that you get complimented on all the time, consider turning it into a side hustle to generate some additional income.

The lesson here is that you can't predict when a recession will happen. Yes, there are typically signals for when a recession is on the horizon, but that doesn't often give you enough time to pay off your debts and boost your savings. The best way to recession-proof your wealth is to start in on these steps as soon as possible. The further ahead you're prepared, the better off you will be, meaning you will be able to come out of a recession without any major losses or any significant debt. Practicing sound financial decision-making from the start will enable you to prepare for the inevitable and allow your money to work for you.

Take Action

Put some time on your calendar to lay out a plan for each of the five areas in this section to help you recession-proof your finances. Review the progress you have made throughout this book. Make sure you have created a plan that includes these steps:

- Bulk up your emergency savings.
- Create your plans to pay off debt.
- Diversify your investments.
- Become BFFs with your budget.
- Create multiple streams of income.

Recession-Proof Jobs and Businesses

Jobs and businesses that are recession-proof are typically stable and can thrive even during economic downturns. While certain industries like hospitality, tourism, and some retail sectors are closely linked to economic conditions, there are other jobs and businesses that remain relatively unaffected by the state of the economy.

They are usually tied to things people need or deal with every day, like food and healthcare, which they'll still spend money on even in tough times. Although no job or business is 100% guaranteed, recession-proof jobs and businesses are a good bet for anyone looking for a job or looking to start a business or side hustle that's more likely to stay stable regardless of what's happening in the economy.

Recession-Proof Job Ideas

If you are curious about what types of jobs weather recessions the best or you are interested in a career change, here are some great recession-proof job ideas and a brief description of what each entails:

- **IT professionals:** They are responsible for designing, implementing, and managing computer systems and networks, ensuring smooth operations, troubleshooting issues, and maintaining security measures.
- **Software developers:** They create applications, programs, and systems for computers and mobile devices, addressing user needs, designing software solutions, coding, and testing software functionality.
- **Medical and healthcare providers:** This includes doctors, nurses, physician assistants, dentists, therapists, and more. They diagnose, treat, and care for patients in various healthcare settings, promoting overall health and wellness.
- **Pharmacists and pharmacy technicians:** They give medications, provide guidance on their usage, and ensure prescriptions are correct, while pharmacy technicians support pharmacists in tasks like prescription filling and customer interaction.
- **Accounting and bookkeeping professionals:** They manage financial records, prepare tax returns, and offer financial advice, helping clients to track their finances, analyze their data, and make informed financial decisions.
- **Utility workers:** For example, electricians, plumbers, and HVAC technicians. They install, repair, and maintain essential utility systems like electricity, water, heating, and cooling to ensure functionality and safety.
- **Public safety workers:** This includes law enforcement, firefighters, and EMTs. They protect communities, respond to emergencies, enforce laws, provide medical aid, and promote overall public safety.
- **Government workers:** They serve various roles in the government like handling education, healthcare, law

enforcement, transportation, and social services at the federal, state, or local levels.

- **Education professionals:** For example, teachers, professors, special education teachers, coaches, and tutors. They educate students (children, teens, or adults), develop curriculum plans, instruct classes or programs, assess progress, and support student learning and development in academic institutions.
- **Senior care providers:** This includes caregivers, nurses, and assisted living staff. They provide care and support to elderly individuals, assisting them with daily tasks, monitoring their health, administering medications, and ensuring a safe environment.
- **Delivery and courier services:** They transport goods between locations, managed by delivery drivers, couriers, and logistics professionals who oversee shipping, tracking, and efficient delivery processes.
- **Legal professionals:** They help people navigate the complex world of law. They provide legal advice, represent clients in court, conduct legal research, draft legal documents, and negotiate on their behalf.
- **Social workers:** They work to address social and emotional challenges for individuals, families, and communities. They offer counseling, support services, and advocacy, as well as guidance on accessing various support resources.
- **Financial advisors, planners, and counselors:** They assist with financial management, goal setting, investment strategies, and financial education.
- **Veterinarians:** They diagnose and treat animal illnesses and injuries, perform surgeries, prescribe medications, and promote animal health and welfare.
- **Insurance agents:** They assess insurance needs, explain coverage options, process applications, and assist clients with claims and policy management.

- **Customer service representatives in essential industries:** They support customers with inquiries, complaints, and requests. They also provide information, resolve issues, process orders, and ensure positive customer experiences. Essential industries include healthcare, food, transportation, financial services, communications, education, and more.

Recession-Proof Business Ideas

If you are considering recession-proof side hustles or business ideas, below are some industries where businesses thrive despite economic downturns by catering to essential needs and consumer priorities (more on side hustles in the next chapter):

- **Baby products and childcare:** Businesses that cater to babies and children, such as clothing, essentials, and childcare, remain stable because parents prioritize their children's needs regardless of economic conditions.
- **Food and drinks, groceries:** Food and beverage businesses, grocery services, and essential food delivery services are recession-proof as people prioritize food and household necessities regardless of economic fluctuations.
- **Healthcare and senior services:** Businesses catering to seniors (e.g. home care and caregiver services) always have an ongoing demand for services to assist with basic needs and daily tasks among the elderly population.
- **Educational services:** Business in tutoring, online learning, and educational materials thrive as people invest in learning and skill development during economic challenges.
- **Technology services:** Software development, IT services, and electronics are always necessary as businesses and individuals rely on technology for communication, work, and entertainment.
- **Repair services:** Repair businesses, such as automotive repair shops, appliance repair services, and home

maintenance, remain stable as people prefer repairing essentials over buying new ones during tough times.

- **Pet care:** Pet grooming, pet supplies, and pet care services are recession-proof because pet owners prioritize their pets' care and well-being regardless of economic challenges.
- **Cleaning services:** Residential cleaning, commercial janitorial services, and specialized cleaning businesses stay in demand as businesses, healthcare facilities, and households still require cleaning services to maintain safe and healthy environments.
- **Digital marketing:** Digital marketing agencies, social media consultants, and online advertising thrive as other businesses will continue invest in digital presence and marketing strategies to reach customers effectively.
- **Beauty, skincare, and personal wellness:** Beauty services and cosmetic and wellness products can be resilient as people continue to prioritize self-care even during tough economic times.
- **Freelance services and agencies:** During recessions, many employers turn to freelancers and freelance agencies as an alternative to hiring full-time employees.

Exploring recession-proof jobs and businesses can offer you stability and peace of mind, especially in uncertain economic times because they tend to ride out economic ups and downs and they provide steady income as well as room for growth. And so they are valuable options to consider as you work on your financial wellness and building wealth.

Take Action

If you're interested in a career shift or are brainstorming side hustle or business ideas, take some time out to explore and research various recession-proof job and business ideas. Use the job and business ideas examples provided in this section as a starting point.

MEET ASHLEE SANG

Ashlee is the founder of Ashlee Sang Consulting (AshleeSang .com), through which she equips conscious and caring leaders to take confident, meaningful action in alignment with their values. She is also the host of the *Purpose & Progress Podcast.*

For several years, Ashlee worked as a freelancer as she prepared herself for full-time entrepreneurship, alongside being a wife and mother. She practices conscious consumerism and shares the key tips she has leveraged to successfully navigate her personal and business finances despite various seasons of challenging economic times.

How do you approach financial decisions personally and in your business during tough economic times, given your personal focus on conscious consumerism?

> Your values impact your money. They're a direct reflection of how you price, how you spend, and who you trust to invest with in terms of service providers or brands. Basically, your values shape every decision you make – financial and otherwise. Or at least any decision that feels good in the end, even if it's hard along the way. So I spend a lot of time researching brands and their claims, supply chains, content, and company ethos. I also have go-to sources I trust, like bloggers and YouTubers who do even more research than I have time for and have relationships and conversations with brands that I wouldn't be able to access as an individual consumer, so that's a shortcut to choosing a values-aligned option.
>
> But my biggest personal "hack" for not only saving an extreme amount of money but also guaranteeing that I'm not contributing negatively to people's lives or the planet is to shop secondhand. I love the idea of

items having a story or past life (even when they're new with tags, which is common!). I know I'm saving materials from going to the landfill. And I don't have to be as picky about the brand because my dollars aren't supporting their operations or vision – it's already a sunk cost.

Can you share some tips or strategies that have worked well for you in maintaining financial stability and growth for your business and personal finances during challenging economic periods?

I track my income and expenses in both my personal and business finances religiously. I've been doing this since I was maybe five years old and got a "play" checkbook, which I used to balance my allowance and enter the receipts I got from shopping and so on. This was one of the best things my parents did to increase my financial literacy and awareness and I'm eager to do something similar with my kids.

I also started doing a net worth review at the end of every month to be able to get a full view of all our investments and savings in a single place since I have so many different accounts on different timelines and things I don't touch on the daily, like a high-yield savings account, health savings accounts (HSAs), and our mutual funds and ETFs. This gives me a better picture of how we're doing, even when our normal checking account is running low or it's a low-revenue month in my business.

Balancing roles as a wife, mother, and entrepreneur while managing finances can be tricky. How do you handle this juggling act?

This is an area I can continue to improve on because I still think of them as quite siloed, but I know I would benefit from aligning my business income goals with my life goals. That way, it would make achieving them more focused and meaningful. I view my business first and foremost as being responsible for its own expenses, and then leverage any overflow to bolster our personal projects.

I often do big lump-sum transfers from my business to our personal account when we want to invest in a high-yield savings account or health savings account, send money to Senegal (where my husband is from) to build on the properties we've bought, take a special or more experimental investment opportunity, or just refill our personal coffers if they're low for whatever reason.

I also have a few investment accounts for both of my kids so that we're creating a legacy for them. They'll eventually be responsible for saving a percentage of their money and/or investing some as well so that they're part of that legacy-building.

We have a fully shared financial situation in our household. I manage the money and my husband now makes more of it with this current phase of life with small kids, but we make decisions on where to spend the big collective pool together.

What is your best strategy for managing your personal and business finances during economic downturns?

My biggest strategy for economic downturns is to keep a nest egg, for both my personal and business finances, but especially because my business tends to have much more unpredictable or inconsistent earnings.

This is because: (a) this approach is practical. The expenses keep coming, whether the income or business revenue does or not. Both recurring and one-off annual costs hit on their own schedule, not based on when you want to pay them. And (b) it's reassuring to know that if an opportunity pops up or my business revenue is down that month or quarter, I won't be left scrambling.

Based on your experiences, what is the top piece of advice you would give to help others navigate their finances successfully during tough economic climates?

I'm not a huge fan of "best practices" because I feel most of us and our needs are so specific, but one piece of advice that's universally applicable is to keep tabs on your money. You don't need to be stressed or checking your balances constantly, but check in weekly, or at least monthly.

Track all the little and big income and expenses. Know when all the big purchases (property taxes, semi-annual insurance payments, business license and software renewals, etc.) are coming down the pike since that'll disrupt your normal spending patterns and budget.

Be aware of subscriptions or other expenses you're paying for but not using. Plan for the unexpected (basement flood, popped tires, clients drying up for a period of time).

This careful, incremental diligence makes both the details and the big picture cleaner to track, easier for taxes, and gives an at-a-glance-view of how much money your business and household really have on hand. So then when times get extra hard, you'll know where you have wiggle room to "tighten the belt" and where you don't need to worry or change unnecessarily.

CHAPTER 8
Making More Money

Don't wait – create your own opportunities.

NEGOTIATING TO WIN

Your salary is essentially the baseline of how much you'll earn over the course of your lifetime, and how much you start with is incredibly important – especially because any raises or bonuses you receive are typically a percentage of your base salary. In this chapter, I'll be breaking down key steps you can take to earn you more money using the power of negotiation.

As women, we are often guilty of not asking for what we deserve – especially in the workplace. We are also guilty of not negotiating compensation when we're offered a new job. In fact, statistics show that women are leaving behind between $1 million and $1.5 million of lifetime earnings due to not negotiating their salaries or asking for raises![1] Now that's crazy.

When I graduated from college and got my first job, my starting salary was $54,000. I was ecstatic. It was more money than I'd ever earned in my life, and as far I was concerned, I was balling. It didn't once cross my mind to ask for more money or even a signing bonus. I was just happy I got a job.

Well, as time went by and I got to know my coworkers, I realized that I was the lowest earner in the entire group, despite all being hired for the same position – and despite the fact that we all had similar educational backgrounds.

Some of them made thousands of dollars more than I did, while others had gotten signing bonuses. Why? Because unlike me, they didn't accept the first offer they received. Instead, they asked for more. Not only did asking for more get them more money, but it also positioned them to earn more when it came time for raises and bonuses, since those are given as a percentage of the base salary. Over the course of their careers, that's likely hundreds of thousands of dollars more than I'd make.

[1]"Research Shows Not Negotiating Your Salary Could Cost You $1 Million (Especially Women)," https://www.inc.com/jeff-haden/research-shows-not-negotiating-your-salary-could-cost-you-1-million-especially-.html.

That experience lit a fire in me to step out of my comfort zone and get what I knew I was worth going forward. And so, knowing what I know now, being older and wiser, I have four quick tips to help you become a better negotiator and get what you are truly worth:

- **Don't be afraid to ask.** Fear is the number-one reason we don't ask for more money – but what are we really afraid of? The worst thing that could possibly happen is that the request is rejected, and that's it. So instead of being afraid or intimidated, come up with a plan on how to make your request.

  Practice your spiel in front of the mirror, type it up and read it out loud, and then ask yourself, "What's the worst thing that could possibly happen?" Understanding that your request for a raise is not a life-or-death matter will help you put things in perspective and put your fear back in its place.

  With each new job I got, not only did I negotiate my base salary, but I also negotiated other benefits as well, including more vacation days, the option to work from home, a better work computer, and even a better ergonomic office chair! The worst response I got was "no" and so I would simply shelve my request and revisit it a few months later after I had accomplished something big at work.

TIP

If you're turned down for a request at work, whether it's a raise or something else, ask for feedback so you can understand why your request was denied and use this information to improve in order to strengthen your case the next time you ask.

- **Treat your request like a business transaction.** As women, we tend to tie our emotions to the things that go on in our lives, including our careers and asking for raises. When our emotions are involved, we sometimes show vulnerability or look like we are complaining because we've associated our feelings with the situation. Keep in mind that a request for a raise might not come across the way you want it to.

  To get around this, know that it's all about your delivery. When you make your request, don't make any excuses or complaints. Instead, think of it as a business transaction – present your case and why you deserve a raise, talk about your accomplishments, and keep it strictly business. Try as much as you can to keep your emotions and complaints to a minimum.

  For me, it helped to schedule a formal meeting with my boss to have these kinds of conversations. Beforehand, I would outline my talking points so I could come into the meeting prepared to have a focused discussion.
- **Leverage what makes you unique and valuable.** Know your professional worth and capitalize on it! When you make your request, talk about the value you've brought to the company. Remind your boss what you've accomplished, created, or improved and the success that your work has driven. When you present your case this way, they'll be hard-pressed to turn you down.

  So start keeping a list of all your accomplishments and successes at work, no matter how small. This way, when it comes time to speak with your boss or complete a self-assessment, you have this list of all the great work you've done as a reference.
- **Do your research.** When asking for a raise, it's important to be realistic. Do your research and understand what the industry averages are for your role and location. Don't expect to be given anything if you don't know what you're

worth. But also, be sure you're not asking for a salary fit for a major city if you're in a small town. With each new job I got, I also made sure to ask what it would take for me to qualify for the next highest possible raise and the highest possible bonus when the time for raises and bonuses came around, so I knew what to focus on and where to improve.

My friend Dorianne St. Fleur, an HR expert, career coach, and the founder of yourcareergirl.com, suggests keeping the answers to the following questions in mind when it comes to negotiating the salary you deserve:

- Have you done your research so you're clear on competitive salary? (Glassdoor, LinkedIn, and word of mouth are good resources for this.)
- Have you identified your acceptable and aspirational numbers when it comes to your salary range?
- Are there other areas besides salary you want to negotiate, like paid time off or working from home?
- Have you identified what is completely nonnegotiable for you?
- Are you prepared to explain why you're qualified for your target salary?
- Have you thought about your next steps if your terms aren't met? Will you walk away, ask for a trial period, or start looking for a new job?

In addition to becoming a better negotiator, you also want to be able to navigate around financial pitfalls as you make progress in your career. In her experience as an HR expert, Dorianne has identified five major salary mistakes that can set women back financially.

Mistake #1: Not having a compensation strategy.

A compensation strategy is a plan that spells out your long-term salary expectations. These expectations are based on skill level and experience, industry standards for people in similar positions, and unique value. Basically, you calculate your worth, add tax, and create a plan to get you to that dollar amount.

While it would be great to have a compensation strategy before you start your first job – your initial salary creates the baseline for what you'll be paid in your lifetime – this is something most women simply don't know they should do. A lot of us, especially those fresh out of college and excited just to have a job, don't take the time to think strategically about how much we get paid – which ends up being a costly mistake.

If you don't already have a compensation strategy, start now. Take out a pen and paper and think about where you are now, where you actually should be, and where you want to be in the future. Once you've done the math, create a plan to get there – whether that's by asking for a raise, looking for a new job, or starting a side hustle.

Mistake #2: Assuming you'll be paid for your contributions.

It sounds so simple, right? Do a good job at work and you'll eventually get paid for it. However, this isn't always the case. While there are times when doing your job well can mean a few extra coins, 9 times out of 10 managers aren't sitting around waiting to hand over wads of cash every time you accomplish a new goal.

Instead of passively waiting to be paid for your contributions, realize that you'll need to be an active participant in your salary progression. If you expect to be recognized financially for what you do at work, you'll need to make sure your boss (and anyone else involved in money decisions) is well aware of that.

Whether you have to beef up your annual self-evaluation or schedule a stand-alone meeting to talk about your achievements, you need to make sure you create a platform to show your boss all you've accomplished throughout the year.

Mistake #3: Being uncomfortable talking about money.

Many women have pushed the subject of money to a space that is "off limits," unable to discuss things like current salary, future financial goals, and earning potential with even their closest friends. So to bring up the subject to their boss – to express dissatisfaction with their salary and ask for a raise – can cause a lot of anxiety.

Although it can be tough, it's time to move past the uneasiness that comes with talking about money – especially if you actually want to earn more. The saying "A closed mouth won't get fed" couldn't be truer in this situation.

The most important conversations are usually the ones that are most uncomfortable, so it's definitely in your best interest to push past your fear and have it anyway.

Mistake #4: Making emotional decisions.

Making any decision when you're in your feelings is a bad idea. Emotions like anxiety, anger, nervousness, and fear can sabotage your efforts to get the raise you want. So keep those emotions in check! Being so nervous that you accept the first lowball offer you get or so angry that you yell at your boss when talking about how much you deserve a higher salary will essentially ruin any chance of a positive outcome.

Your goal should be to remain calm and collected throughout the entire process, leaving the way you feel out of the equation. When it comes to making decisions on salary, focus on your research and the facts.

Mistake #5: Being afraid to walk away.

Even if you create the right compensation strategy, ensure your manager is aware of your contributions, get comfortable talking about money, and leave your emotions out of your decision-making process, the final decision on whether you ultimately get that raise is out of your control.

Instead of getting hung up on this fact, have a contingency plan and exit strategy in case things don't work the way you would have liked. You know what's worse than realizing you're being underpaid? Realizing you're being underpaid, asking for what you deserve, and then staying put if nothing changes. This fear of change is what holds many women back in forging a new career path for themselves.

Take Action

Prepare for your next salary negotiation conversation with the tips Dorianne has provided to help you have a successful conversation and outcome:

1. Do your research so you're clear on competitive salaries. You can use sites like Glassdoor and LinkedIn or ask people you know who are in similar industries.
2. Identify your acceptable and aspirational numbers when it comes to your salary range.
3. Determine any other areas besides salary you want to negotiate, like paid time off or working from home.
4. Be sure to identify what is completely nonnegotiable for you.
5. Be prepared to explain why you're qualified for your target salary.
6. Determine what your next steps will be if your terms aren't met.

MEET STEPH MAY

Steph is a mother of two beautiful girls and lives in Naarm (Melbourne), Wurundjeri Country, Australia. She considers herself fortunate to work in a field she is passionate about and feels very much on purpose working as a Director of Programs and Outcomes with a First Nations not-for-profit in Australia.

Steph is an avid Clever Girl Finance community member who shares how she adjusted her mindset and leveraged goal setting to get promoted at work to a director role, increase her income, and start achieving her financial goals.

What steps did you take to begin adjusting your mindset in terms of growing in your career and achieving your financial goals?

> The first step I took was reading the first edition of this book – *Clever Girl Finance: Ditch Debt, Save Money, and Build Real Wealth* – a few years ago! The value for me came from what I learned in this book and then discovering the wealth of resources available from Clever Girl Finance, including the other books, videos on YouTube, podcasts, and the weekly money newsletters. I started reading other personal finance books as well and began listening to the *Clever Girls Know Podcast* at least once week.
>
> I loved reading about and listening to other people's stories and hearing diverse life experiences that challenged my views. That consistency, and the regularity of exposing myself to various resources, helped shift my mindset from one of scarcity to believing that I could achieve financial well-being.
>
> I then started keeping a spreadsheet where I recorded all the actions I was taking as it related to my financial well-being. This was a really good way for me to track my progress. In addition, I kept a detailed record of my weekly expenditure, which I would write down in a book. I reviewed my expenditure, looked for any trends, and I would make a commitment to myself to take further action from there if I noticed anything that could be improved. For example, I realized I was spending too much money on treats for my kids, so instead I opted to give my youngest daughter $5 a week for her treats, which set a boundary and created a fixed budget for that spending.
>
> I've continued tracking my actions and expenditures to this day by making sure I set aside time each week

for my "financial well-being." The other things I did to maintain a growth mindset included writing down my goals and putting them on the door of my wardrobe where I could easily mark my progress for each goal. For example, I was able to fully fund my emergency savings account.

From a career perspective, one thing that really helped me adjust my mindset was joining an annual goal-setting call hosted by Bola and the Clever Girl Finance team. I found this session so motivating and it was then that I wrote down my goal of wanting to get promoted to a director role at my job. I think the key mindset shift here was that I gave myself permission to have this dream and I acknowledged it. There was a role advertised at the time and so I took a very brave step and applied for the role. Whilst I didn't get the role at that time, I do believe I set the wheels in motion to eventually be offered the role later in the same year.

How did you create goals that aligned with your career aspirations and financial objectives?

I got very specific about my goals. I also took the advice not to have too many goals so I wouldn't get overwhelmed, and I ensured that my goals felt ambitious but would be achievable.

I'd known for a long time that I was great at my job, but I hadn't really advanced into more senior roles. After the Clever Girl Finance annual goal-setting session, I got really clear about wanting to move into a leadership role. This decision was partly about earning a higher salary, but more about addressing my limiting beliefs and imposter syndrome, where I'd told myself that I wasn't the right fit and there were people more deserving than me. I also wanted to build a three-month emergency fund and make contributions to increase my superannuation (retirement funds) account balance as part of my journey to achieving financial well-being.

As mentioned earlier, I had a visual tool that was a simple little chart on the door of my wardrobe where I'd color in $1,000 increments as I saved money. It was fun to do and gave me a sense of achievement. Now that I have achieved my goals I feel so proud of myself. I really have come so far.

What specific things did you do to demonstrate your value at work to position yourself for your promotion to director and the accompanying salary increase?

There were roles at my organization that were being advertised both internally and externally. I thought very hard about applying for one of the advertised roles but talked myself out of it as I thought that the organization already had someone in mind. It wasn't until after the goal-setting session that I realized I needed to apply for one of the advertised roles, with the objective of shifting my mindset to see myself as a potential candidate and to allow my organization to recognize me and consider me as a potential candidate.

The initial work was with myself and my mindset, no one was going to see my leadership potential if I didn't see it in myself! So I wrote a great application, and I got an interview. In preparation for my interview, I listened to YouTube clips on public speaking, I wrote out possible interview questions and I practiced being interviewed. I also dressed for success so they could see me as someone who could represent the organization at various meetings and forums that the director-level role would attend. I did not get the job at that time, but I was able to put myself and my resume in front of senior leadership. By being interviewed I had the opportunity to showcase my range of experience as well as show my initiative.

Later in the year, I was offered the opportunity to act in a senior role for a few weeks. That was another very important opportunity for me to test the role out and for the organization to test me and see how I performed. I loved it! I not only knew that I could I do the job, but I knew it would be very rewarding for me. It wasn't too long after that I was offered a permanent position. I realize now that I was quite bored in my previous role, and I wasn't learning or growing much. I've now been in my new position for about seven months, and I love it. I'm learning new skills, and I'm learning to lead others and delegate. Its challenging but incredibly rewarding.

Did you feel any doubts along the way, and how did you maintain a positive mindset?

Yes, absolutely! I felt scared and I felt like I wasn't deserving of the opportunity. I worried that the organization's leader would think poorly of me because I didn't let them know of my interest prior to applying. The imposter syndrome kicked in! I think I had to treat it a bit like a game in the end and play my best cards. I gave myself a break by telling myself that it didn't matter if I didn't get the role and even if it took me 5, 10, or more applications to get a director-level position – this would be practice, I would learn from the experience, and it would inform my future applications. Just having the courage to apply for the position was a big thing for me. I acknowledged and celebrated myself for that.

How important was networking and building relationships in your journey toward your career advancement?

Networking has been super-important for me. I have been working in the same field for 12 years now and I'm well known in this field. I have built up my subject matter expertise. I have lots of great relationships and a good reputation. In fact, I was working at a job I really loved prior to coming to my current organization. I wasn't looking for a new job, but a senior member of the organization called me and told me about the job and asked me if I would be interested in applying and said that I would be a great fit.

This happened because of the relationships I had built over time and it set the wheel in motion for later events. I am so lucky that I work with wonderful people in a field I am very passionate about. I feel very much on purpose with the work I do, and people see that.

How did achieving this promotion and salary increase contribute to your overall financial goals, and what steps did you take to start achieving those goals?

My personal growth and has been profound. My salary has also risen significantly. With the new director role, my salary has increased by 55% in just over two years – that is amazing! This salary increase has allowed me to achieve my financial goals much more quickly!

A few weeks before I knew I would be offered the director role, I decided to separate from my then partner. I was worried about how I could afford to live on my own with my kids. Serendipitously, it was just a few weeks later that I received the call about a new role. Now just over two years later I am in a much better financial position. I couldn't have imagined this at the time I decided to separate from my partner.

My financial goals now include being mortgage free, and ensuring my retirement is comfortable; as soon as I could, I began co-contributing to my superannuation and I've used online calculators to work out what I need. Every three months I look at my net worth and it is really cool to see the increase in my savings.

I had a short-term goal to send my eldest daughter on an exchange program overseas. This had been a dream of mine since I had her. I didn't have the opportunity to do this as a student because my parents couldn't afford it as it was too expensive! So, to realize that dream, I continued to live with my ex-partner for six months after we separated (we remained on good terms) so I could save money for my daughter's exchange program as well as save enough money to move out.

Some of the other steps I've taken have been to create a comprehensive budget and set up bank accounts for my emergency and sinking funds. I am so grateful for the advice and support offered through Clever Girl Finance.

What advice would you give to individuals aspiring to get promoted at work, increase their income significantly, and make progress toward their financial objectives?

You can do it and you deserve it! Be brave with setting your goals and then break them down to smaller achievable steps. Finally, surround yourself with a supportive community – Clever Girl Finance is great for that!

SIDE HUSTLES

Wouldn't it be nice to make some extra cash on the side each month on top of your current income? Well, I'm a huge fan of side hustles because they help increase your income, which allows you to pay off your debts faster so you can save and invest more.

I've had a side hustle for as long as I can remember. From selling Avon to my mom's friends to having an online retail business to being a successful part-time wedding photographer, my side hustles have been pivotal in accomplishing several of my financial goals.

In fact, I started Clever Girl Finance as a side hustle while still working full-time in my technology career and running said wedding photography business! Today, I run Clever Girl Finance full-time.

The great thing about having a side hustle is that making money on the side does not always have to involve a full-blown small business. You can easily make more money doing things you are skilled at or leveraging resources you already have. Then you can put those extra funds toward saving, investing, or debt repayment – not bad, huh?

That said, it's important that you have the right mindset as you approach setting up or growing your side hustle. Working on a side hustle takes time, hard work, and openness to learning new things, and sometimes you'll find that you need to pivot. Having the right mindset is what will keep you motivated and focused, especially as you work to get your business on its feet.

You'll also need to remind yourself of your *why*: your reason for wanting to achieve your financial goals. Because the money you earn from your side hustle can help you accelerate achieving those financial goals, but you need to be committed to doing the work. The good news is that if you are reading this, you have what it takes!

Ideas for a Side Hustle

The number-one question I get from people interested in starting a side hustle is usually around what type of business they should be doing. One of the lowest-barrier-to-entry side hustles is monetizing your driving skills and car by driving for Uber or Lyft after work or on the weekends, or by doing deliveries with Instacart. These are considered side hustles since they are based on your schedule and when you want to earn the extra income. They are also easy to start because you don't need a website, and you won't be selling a specific product or service directly to customers. The companies behind these services help you manage all the logistics through their apps so you can get started easily.

Some popular ideas for successful side hustles where you offer a specific product or service include selling physical goods online through Etsy, eBay, or Amazon; offering services like coaching, consulting, or tutoring; or selling digital products like e-books and online courses.

While those might be the most popular, there are many other options, including those in the real world (i.e. not just online). For example, you could become a freelancer if you have skills like coding, design, writing, editing, and more. Another idea could be starting a home-based service like baking or catering. There are so many ideas to start a side hustle – you just need to narrow down what you're good at and what you like doing. (You can also go back to reference the recession-proof business ideas I mentioned in Chapter 7.)

If you're unsure, asking yourself the following questions can help you narrow down your side hustle ideas:

- What are my passions and interests, and can I turn them into a viable side hustle?
- What problems or needs do I see around me that I could solve by creating a product or service?
- How can I leverage my skills, knowledge, and experience to create value for others and generate income?
- What feedback or insights have I received from friends, family, or colleagues that could spark a side hustle idea?

Once you have an idea to pursue, you need a plan. Real success with a side hustle comes with having a strategy to help your business succeed. Yes, having great products or a great service is key to making sales, but there are five foundational things you need to have in place in order to establish a model that will help your business become successful:

1. **A clear plan for running your hustle.** Having a clear model for your side hustle helps you understand and lay out how much time in your schedule you can dedicate to your side hustle, how exactly you intend to deliver value with your products and services, and the type of experience you plan to provide your ideal customer. For instance, if your side hustle is based on a luxury brand you have created, a few important questions you'd want to ask yourself include: Are your products packaged in a way that aligns with the luxury experience you want your customers to have? What about your website – is it in line with your brand? Also, what systems or people do you have in place to help deliver the experience you are offering?

   Your operating model will help ensure you are delivering what you promise your customers. In addition, once your operating model is fine-tuned and running, it will allow you to scale your business because you'll have a well-established process in place.

2. **Your plan to make money.** One of your major goals as a business owner is to turn a profit. Obviously, you can't turn a profit if you don't have a means of earning income, so creating a plan to generate revenue will be key. This means outlining the products and services you plan to sell and exactly how you will communicate those products and services to potential customers. It also means fine-tuning your revenue stream as you learn what's working and what isn't.

   Keep in mind that customers will buy your product or service because it solves a problem or a need they have, and so you want your product or service not only to solve their problem but also to deliver a great experience or result. If done the right way, you'll likely have return customers, and very importantly your existing customers will tell other people, share on social media, and/or leave great reviews, which in turn can help you make more money.

Once you have a solid revenue stream in place, it becomes so much easier to forecast your business earnings and profitability.

3. **Your profits.** After you subtract the cost of creating your goods and any additional overhead from the price you are charging, how much do you have left? Becoming profitable is great, but ideally, you want to have a clear understanding of exactly how much profit you are generating on each product or service you offer.

   You can then assess how to maximize your profitability by reducing your costs or competitively increasing your prices – or both.

4. **Your startup costs and operating expenses.** Your startup costs are the costs that you'll incur to get your side hustle up and running. They are typically one-time expenses related to things like getting a new website designed, registering your domain name, registering your business, buying equipment like a computer, getting licenses, and the like.

   Your operating expenses, on the other hand, are basically how much money you need to keep your business running day to day. How much do you need to cover your recurring expenses like Internet hosting fees, utilities, insurance, tool subscriptions, supplies, inventory, shipping costs, and contractors? These costs would need to be laid out as part of your operating expenses and will give you a baseline of how much you'll need each month to keep your business going. Note that some of your operating expenses may be fixed (e.g. hosting fees and Internet service), while other expenses may be variable (e.g. product materials and production costs).

It's also a good idea to lay out exactly how you will fund your business now and in the future – and what you'll need to have in place to obtain the necessary funding.

5. **A solid business budget and tracking your cash flow.** Having a solid budget for your business is essential to the financial success of your business. Your budget basically allows you to plan for your upcoming expenses, manage your finances properly, and stay on top of your expenses as they occur. Tracking your side hustle revenue is also known as your cash flow and it is essentially the revenue you earn from your side hustle as well as the expenses you incur running it. You have positive cash flow when your revenue exceeds your expenses. On the other hand, negative cash flow happens when your expenses are greater than your revenue. So the biggest things you want to track are your revenue and your operating expenses.

   Not only will your budget help you track the overall health of your business finances, but it can also give you pretty good insights around your profits and losses.

If set up and executed properly, a side hustle can be a great boost to your income while you pursue your interests at the same time. If you have an idea, lay it out and consider starting your own side hustle. Be sure to do the necessary research to create a strategy you can follow and stay on top of your business finances – this is key!

TIP

When you're juggling a side hustle, managing your time well is key. So figure out what work really matters for your bottom line and prioritize those things. Leverage tools like calendars and to-do lists to stay organized and say no to things that are not a good use of your time.

Take Action

In order to establish a successful side hustle, here are two things to get in place to help you create your strategy, keeping the tips I mentioned above in mind:

1. A business plan highlighting what your business is about, what products and services you will offer, who your ideal customer is, how you plan to fund it, and how you will drive sales
2. A business budget to help you map out your start-up costs, your recurring monthly expenses and to track your cash flow (See the appendix for simple startup expenses and side hustle budget templates.)
   - To start, you can structure your business budget to include how much money you have to set up your side hustle (if you are just getting started) or all your sources of revenue (if you are up and running).
   - You'll also need to include your fixed expenses like Internet hosting, tool subscriptions, and so on, and your variable expenses, like cost of materials, shipping costs, and the like.
   - You can then start tracking your total revenue and your total expenses to determine your profit or loss each month.
   - Don't forget to create line items in your budget to set aside funds for taxes once you become profitable, savings, and emergencies.

MEET LUCILLE ROACHE

Lucille Roache is a business coach (AssetBusinessConsultancy .co.uk), an author, and a trainer. She helps new and growing service-based business owners to identify and attract the right clients, create attractive offers, and market those offers in a way that aligns with their strengths.

Based on her personal experience with coaching others as well as with starting and running her own side hustles, Lucille shares key tips on how to generate recurring income with your side hustle.

Can you share some key tips from your personal experience on how to generate recurring income with a side hustle?

> The best way to have recurring revenue is with a sales funnel. A sales funnel is a strategy that you use to bring new people into your world so you can sell your products and services to them.
>
> The first step is to let people know that you exist. Social media is a great tool for visibility and to raise awareness of what you do. Once people know that you exist, the next step is to give them something that they're interested in. If you sell digital products, this could be a free gift that's connected to the paid product that you offer.
>
> So, for example, if you're a website designer, you could create a free guide that details the five "must have" pages every service-based business owner needs to have on their website. In exchange for this free gift, people give you their name and email address and you can add them to your email list. Once they're on your list you send them an automated series of emails that helps your audience get to know you better, and then you finish with a paid offer. This process can be automated so you have a system that can generate recurring revenue.

What are some effective strategies for identifying and attracting the right clients for a side hustle or small business, especially for those starting a side hustle for the first time?

You first need to know and understand the desires of your ideal client; what is it that they want more than anything else? To use the website designer example again, you would ask: What is it that somebody who wants a website desires more than anything? Are they ultimately looking for a website that's going to help them convert clients, promote their shop, or generate leads?

Once you understand this desire you can speak to it in your content and ensure that you're creating offers that match the needs of your ideal client. If you don't know the desires of your ideal client, survey them and ask them what their desires are!

What are some key financial considerations that entrepreneurs should keep in mind when starting and running a side hustle?

Startup costs can be quite expensive, especially when you're not yet making any money in your business. So the best place to start is to make a list of all the tools, resources, and equipment you'll need to get started in business. Then make a list of ongoing costs; this could be the cost of a website, and any materials you need to run your business.

At this point you don't need to spend thousands hiring a website designer or getting the best software out there. Start with the basics, then work out how much money you need to make every month to meet each of these expenses.

How can people who are running a side hustle while also working full-time manage their time effectively without burning out?

> My best advice would be to look at the time that you have available. I still do this in my own business. So work out how many hours you work per week and the other things that take up your time, including all your responsibilities. Then review the results and identify how much time you have to spend on your business. For example, it may be two hours in the evenings, or two weekdays and Saturdays.
>
> Once you know how many hours you have, look at the priorities in your business. Your priorities should be the activities that will make you money, like market research and being visible. Things like looking for a logo or spending hours creating a social media post aren't going to make you money. So prioritize the money-making activities in your business and then estimate how much time each activity will take so you can plan your time accordingly and, in turn, avoid burnout.

In your opinion, what are the most common challenges that new and aspiring female entrepreneurs face when starting a side hustle, and what advice would you give on how they can overcome these challenges?

> There are quite a few challenges new business owners face. The first challenge is the temptation just to skip the foundational things like finding out who your ideal client is, doing market research, creating your business plan, and working out your business finances before going straight into marketing your business.

Now the reason this is a challenge is that unless you know whom you're speaking to (i.e. your ideal client), and you understand their needs, it's going to be difficult to market your business because you won't know what to say in your content, what platforms to be on, or what offers to create.

The second biggest challenge is a lack of confidence. It's a lot of pressure to create something that has your name on it and put it out in the world. Sometimes business owners can put too much pressure on themselves and then start to get imposter syndrome and begin doubting their abilities.

To overcome this, make a list of the skills that you have that make you good at what you do. This can include all the training you've done, the work experience you have, and the time you've invested. What this does is provide evidence to your brain to counter the doubts you have.

I also recommend that people keep a brag book of all the compliments or positive feedback you've received from others about the work you do and then when you start to doubt yourself, you can look at this book of evidence to remind you how amazing you are!

CHAPTER 9
Your Self-Care

Self-care and financial wellness go hand in hand. They are both investments in your future prosperity.

#CLEVERGIRLSKNOW

NUTURING YOUR SELF-CARE ALONGSIDE YOUR FINANCIAL WELLNESS. . .BECAUSE YES

Self-care is a crucial yet often overlooked form of wellness that can have a powerful impact on your financial journey. This is simply because if you are struggling mentally, emotionally, or physically, it can be difficult to put in the effort, intention, and focus required to achieve your financial goals.

Think of self-care as your secret weapon for a fulfilling life. When we prioritize our mental, emotional, and physical health, we set ourselves up for success in all areas of our lives, including our finances. On the flipside, neglecting your self-care can lead to burnout, health issues, and financial setbacks.

I've personally gone through seasons of my life where I neglected my self-care, especially as I've built my business. My excuse? I was always too busy and had so much to do (you've probably told yourself this many times as well). Or I would delay practicing self-care, and when I did it would be with the least effort when I knew I needed to do more to take care of myself. Over time, though, I ended up paying for it in the form of burnout and a lack of motivation, and it took me months to recover mentally and emotionally.

And so, as part of updating and expanding this book, I felt it was necessary to include a chapter on self-care, why it's so important that we practice it often, and practical tips I've found helpful in my own life. There will always be more work to do and we can all stay busy, but there is only one you and you need to take care of yourself.

How Self-Care and Your Personal Finances Are Related

Your self-care and your finances are interconnected in so many ways. For instance, by maintaining good physical and mental health through things like exercising regularly, eating a balanced diet, and good stress management, you can minimize the need for medical interventions, and in turn minimize or avoid expensive healthcare costs.

Practicing self-care also means that you are setting boundaries because you are specifically allocating time for rest and relaxation. This can prevent burnout and improve your overall well-being, which can be extremely helpful for focusing on your goals and making sound decisions – including your money goals and financial decisions.

And did you know that practicing self-care can help you avoid impulse spending? That's right! Self-care doesn't mean spending a ton of money on products and fads. In fact, it can help you save. By doing things that make you happy and relaxed, you're less likely to be driven by stress to blow cash on random stuff you never planned to purchase in the first place. It's like your emotions are in check, so your wallet stays in line too.

Plus, being top of your self-care game – taking breaks, getting enough sleep, and not letting stress run your life – can boost your productivity and performance at work or in your business, which can lead to higher income and, when managed correctly, an increased sense of financial stability.

And so, self-care and financial wellness are very much related. It's all about being intentional when it comes to prioritizing your overall well-being and this intention can extend to your personal finances, helping you save, invest, and plan for your future and reduce money-related stress and anxiety along the way.

Simple Self-Care Practices

Now that you know the importance of self-care and how it ties into your personal finances, here are some simple practices I do that you can start implementing as well:

Do a Digital Detox

Give your eyes and mind a break from screens. Schedule regular digital detox sessions so you can reduce your screen time and reconnect with the real world around you. Your brain will thank you for the breather. One way I do this easily is by sometimes leaving my phone at home when I'm going out for a few hours.

Practice Mindfulness

Take a few minutes each day to pause and just be in the moment. Whether it's enjoying your morning coffee, sitting outside on a warm day, or writing in a journal, these little pauses can reset your mind and ease stress.

Get Moving

Find something active that brings you joy. Whether it's dancing in your living room, hiking, or doing yoga, keeping your body active is a win-win for your mood and your health. I try to work out at home three or four times a week and I alternate between strength and cardio. I've found so many great workout channels on YouTube and one of my favorite channels is "Grow with Jo."

Eat Well

Eat meals that keep you full for longer, drink lots of water, and give yourself permission to have that occasional treat you love without feeling guilty. I'm not big on diets or food trends; instead I focus on moderation. I also carry a reusable water bottle with me almost everywhere I go so I'm constantly reminded to drink more water!

Stay Connected

Spending quality time with your friends or family can be a great mood booster. Whether it's a coffee date with a friend or a cozy movie night in with loved ones, these moments are a great to keep your spirit up. Sometimes this can be hard to do, especially if you have a busy or hectic life. That's why I have a monthly calendar reminder on my phone to reach out to a friend I haven't see in a while to schedule a meetup.

Schedule Dedicated "Me Time"

Set aside dedicated time each week for activities that you enjoy and that recharge your batteries. It could be reading a book, taking a long bath, or simply lounging without any distractions. My dedicated me time happens on Fridays. My kids are usually in school, I don't schedule any meetings, and I get to spend time doing simple things that make me happy, like getting a pedicure, taking a long walk, or spending a couple of hours at the bookstore.

Get Enough Sleep

Set a bedtime and stick to it. You can even establish your own bedtime routine. I love to wind down with a warm shower, some skin care, and listening to or reading a good book. It's like a signal to my body that once this happens, bedtime is soon.

Seek Support or Guidance If You Need To

If you're feeling overwhelmed or need extra support, there's absolutely no shame in reaching out to a trusted friend or a professional. Sometimes just being able to share what's weighing you down with someone you trust can help you feel so much better. Therapy can also be a game-changer in helping you navigate life's ups and downs with grace and resilience. Many workplace insurance policies cover therapy, so it's worth exploring.

▶ TIP

Don't overwhelm yourself with too many self-care practices at once – that defeats the purpose! Instead, take your time to figure out and try out the self-care practices that work best for you, and then build them into your schedule.

Don't Forget Gratitude

Being grateful is like having a secret superpower that changes how we see things. When we stop for a second and appreciate what we have, no matter how small, it creates a ripple effect.

Gratitude shifts our mindset and way of thinking from scarcity to abundance. Instead of stressing about what we don't have, it helps us focus on all the amazing things already in our lives. That shift can make us feel content and happy.

Plus, when we're grateful for what we already have, we're likely to be more careful about how we spend our money. We can make better money decisions, cut down on impulse buys, and truly value what we own.

And get this: gratitude isn't just about how it makes us feel; it can also attract positive opportunities and relationships. How, you ask? Well, by practicing gratitude, you are more likely to approach challenges and setbacks with a positive attitude and come up with creative solutions. Gratitude also helps you create a mindset that can recognize opportunities when they come your way, as opposed to dismissing them because you are focused on what you don't have. People also love to be around those who radiate positive energy, and that's exactly what being grateful does for you.

So reminding ourselves to be grateful daily is like unlocking a secret power that brings in a ton of positivity to everything we do. I keep a daily gratitude journal where I write down one to three things that I'm grateful for each day. This exercise makes me pause and think about all the good I have going on in my life each day, which in turn helps me reframe my thinking. It is especially helpful when I've had a rough day. I highly recommend keeping a gratitude list.

Remember, self-care isn't selfish; it's strategic and intentional. By nurturing your well-being, practicing self-care, and cultivating gratitude, you're not just investing in yourself – you're setting the stage for a successful and fulfilling financial and overall life journey.

Take Action

Here are some questions to help you create or assess your self-care practices. Ask yourself, am I:

- Getting enough rest?
- Eating well (i.e. balanced meals)?
- Staying active and incorporating movement into my daily routine?
- Prioritizing my mental wellness?
- Making time for the things that bring me joy?
- Giving myself grace and being self-compassionate?
- Setting boundaries in my relationship and with work to protect my peace?
- Saying no to noncritical commitments that overwhelm me?
- Practicing gratitude?

Also ask yourself:

- What stressors am I currently facing, and how am I managing them?
- What self-care goals and routines do I want to put in place for myself?
- Do I need to seek support or guidance when dealing with challenging emotions or situations?

Based on your answers, create a list of specific actions you can take to take better care of yourself.

CHAPTER 10

Key Financial Actions

STEPS TO KEEP YOUR FINANCIAL PLANS INTACT

You've done it! You made it to the final chapter of this book. Congratulations! You're well on your way to finding financial success.

I've dedicated this last chapter to highlighting the key financial actions you need to take to ensure you continue to improve your finances, accomplish your goals, and move closer to living life on your own terms.

Whether you are single, in a serious relationship, married, changing careers, starting or expanding your family, getting divorced, or caring for elderly parents, there are some key financial actions you should take to ensure you come out on top with your money and are able to meet your financial goals.

This section aggregates a lot of what has been covered throughout this book into useful lists that you can reference when your situation warrants it.

Key financial actions to take if you are employed:

- **Are you saving for retirement?** If your employer offers a retirement savings plan that has a match, you definitely want to take advantage of it by contributing enough to at least get the full match your employer is offering – it's essentially free money. If your employer's plan does not have a match, contribute anyway with a goal to eventually maxing out your contributions. Set up your own IRA through a brokerage and make your retirement contributions that way. The limits are lower, but it's a great start to your long-term retirement savings. In addition, you can start looking into nonretirement investing and repurpose them as investments toward your retirement.
- **Have you set up your emergency fund?** Your first goal should be to get it to $1,000 and then to three to six months of your basic living expenses (food, transportation, and shelter) to ensure you don't have to leverage debt in the event of an unexpected situation.

- **Do you have a debt payoff plan in place?** Start paying off any debt you might have, especially high-interest credit card debt. If you have high-interest debt, get your emergency fund to $1,000 and then focus on getting rid of that debt ASAP. High-interest debt is very expensive – the longer you keep it, the more you pay.
- **Do you have the right kind of insurance?** Review your insurance options to make sure you have the right kind in place (disability, life, health, auto, home, rental, etc.) and update your beneficiaries on all your accounts.

Key financial actions to take if you are married or in a serious relationship:

- **Are you talking to your partner about money frequently?** It's important to communicate about your life and financial goals. Talk about what you'd like to accomplish together and set aside time once a month to go over your progress and review your budget, including your debt repayment, savings, and investment plans.
- **Do you have a joint tax plan in place?** File your taxes together to avoid the penalties of filing separately if you are married. If you file separately, you will pay a higher tax rate and will be unable to claim certain exemptions and deductions. If your preference is to file your taxes separately while you are married, be sure to discuss it with a tax accountant so you are aware of the differences.
- **Is your beneficiary information in place on your accounts and insurance?** If you are married, be sure to update your beneficiary information to include your significant other and dependents.

Key financial actions to take when changing jobs:

- **Have you rolled over your retirement savings from your former employer?** If you've found a new job, don't forget to move your retirement savings plan away from your old employer. Many employers will charge maintenance fees for retirement accounts that belong to former employees. As opposed to rolling your retirement savings into your new employer's plan, consider rolling it into your own IRA through a brokerage firm, as you will have more investment options.

- **Have you set up your retirement savings with your new employer?** Start investing in your new employer's retirement savings plan if they offer one. You don't want to take any unnecessary breaks away from your long-term savings. If your new employer does not offer a plan, you can still contribute to a traditional IRA or Roth IRA independently.
- **Are there gaps in your insurance needs compared to your old employer's plan?** Review your insurance options and adjust accordingly.

Key financial actions to take when expanding your family or if you have children:

- **Are your child's needs included in your monthly budget?** While having children is a blessing, they come with their own expenses, so you want to be sure that you include your child's expenses in your monthly budget.
- **Have you included the cost of a new addition to your budget?** Consider what your costs of having a new baby will be and plan accordingly by saving for your baby's needs in advance of his or her arrival.
- **Have you updated your insurance to include your new addition?** Update your health and life insurance to include your child so they are adequately covered.
- **Does your emergency fund cover your child's essentials?** Be sure to bulk up your emergency fund to include your child's basic needs for three to six months.

- **Do you have your children's college savings plans in place?** You should start saving for their college education now, if possible.

Unfortunately, divorces or the loss of a spouse can happen. While no one hopes for it, it's important to get back on your feet as quickly as possible when it comes to your finances.

Key financial actions to take after a divorce or loss of a spouse:

- **Have you closed joint accounts?** Be sure to close all joint accounts and open new accounts in your own name.
- **Have you updated your beneficiary information?** Update your beneficiaries on all your accounts, including your insurance and retirement savings accounts.
- **Have you created your budget to support yourself as a now-single woman?** Learn how to budget on your own and review your finances on a monthly basis at the very minimum.
- **Have you created an overall financial plan for yourself?** Focus on rebuilding and taking ownership of your finances in their entirety – start budgeting, bulking up your emergency fund, tax planning, and retirement savings.
- **Are you aware of any benefits you are eligible for due to your relationship?** In the case of divorce, are you eligible for child support or alimony? In the case of losing your spouse, are there any Social Security benefits you might be eligible for?
- **Are you aware of the tax implications of inheriting investments?** If you are inheriting any investment or retirement accounts due to the loss of a spouse, make sure you include them in your tax plan for the year.

Key financial actions to take when caring for elderly parents:

- **Have you determined the cost to cover your parents' needs?** Determine what caring for your ageing parents will cost and include it in your financial picture so you are prepared for the expenses you have to pay.

- **Have you determined what benefits they have in place for themselves?** Determine what financial and healthcare options they have in place for themselves, including any Social Security benefits. Then determine if there are any gaps that need to be filled.
- **Have you updated your dependent information?** Update your dependents on your insurance documentation and when you file your taxes.

TIP

If you have dependents, it's a good idea to discuss establishing an estate plan with a financial advisor or estate planning attorney.

Key financial actions to take for your personal wellness:

- **How are you prioritizing your physical health?** This involves eating a healthy diet, ensuring you exercise regularly, and getting enough sleep.
- **What steps are you taking to manage stress and your mental well-being?** Establish a plan to practice mindfulness, engage in activities that bring you joy and relaxation, and create boundaries to protect your peace.
- **Do you have a support system or community that you can lean on for guidance and support?** Prioritize nurturing your meaningful relationships with friends and/or family, stay connected with them, and don't be afraid to seek professional help if needed.
- **Are you consistently practicing gratitude?** Establish the habit of regularly reflecting on and appreciating the positives in your life and the blessings around you.

You can do this through daily journaling, where you write down things you're grateful for, or by expressing gratitude directly to others.

IN CLOSING

You made it! My hope is that by reading this book you are now clear on what you need to do to improve your finances and can start actively working toward your financial goals with all the actionable steps I've laid out.

Keep your copy of this book handy as a reference when certain areas become more applicable to you or for a refresher on what to do when you review your financial plans.

You can also pick up a copy of the accompanying volume, *My Wealth Plan Workbook,* for guidance in creating a personalized financial plan for yourself.

Building wealth takes time, strategy, action, and commitment, and this book provides you with a solid foundation to do just that. While it may take some time, you're well on your way to financial freedom.

Here's to your financial success!

Appendix

PERSONAL BUDGET SPREADSHEET EXCEL

Simple Monthly Personal Budget					
Monthly budget for:					
Income	**Details** (Earned from etc)	**Amount**		**Notes**	
Paycheck Income					
Other Income					
	Total Income				
Category	**Details** (Account names, etc)	**Budgeted Amount**	**Actual Spent**	**Difference** (- under / + over)	**Notes**
Long term / Emergency Savings					
Retirement					
Emergency Fund					
Essentials / Needs					
Mortgage / Rent					
Home Insurance					
Auto Insurance					
Electricity					
Water					
Gas					
Phone					
Groceries					
________					
________					
________					

Debt Payoff	Details (Account names, etc)	Budgeted Amount	Actual Spent	Difference (- under / + over)	Notes
______					
______					
______					
______					
______					
______					
Other Savings & Investments					
College Savings					
______					
______					
______					
Everything Else					
Eating Out					
Travel					
Shopping					
______					
______					
______					
	Total Expenses				
	Total Income - Actual Spent				

 CLEVERGIRLFINANCE.COM

STARTUP EXPENSES

Side Hustle Startup Expenses					
	Startup Expense Type	Category	Description	Estimated Amount	Actual Amount
1					
2					
3					
4					
5					
6					
7					
8					
9					
10					

Total ____________

SIDE HUSTLE BUDGET WORKSHEET

Simple Monthly Side Hustle Budget

	Expense Category	Budgeted	Actual	Difference (-under/+over)
1				
2				
3				
4				
5				
6				
7				
8				
9				
10				

Total ______________________

	Income Category	Estimated	Actual	Difference (-under/+over)
1				
2				
3				
4				
5				
6				
7				
8				
9				
10				

Total ______________________

Monthly Profit or Loss (Income - Expenses)	

Index

A
Abundance, embracing, 25
Active accounts/obligations, organization, 46
Affirmation
  creation, 28–29
  definition, 27
Anger, negative emotion, 21
Annual maintenance fees, 194
Anxiety, negative emotion, 20–21
Applications (apps), usage, 94–95
Assets
  allocation, 180
  increase, 69
Assistance programs, exploration, 114–115
Assessment, execution, 14
Auto insurance, 232–233

B
Backup plan (creation), insurance (usage), 231–237
Bad credit score, rebuilding problem (myth), 220
Bad money habits
  breaking, 57
  identification, 55–61
  impact, 63
Bangura, Esther, 106–109
Bank accounts, organization/tracking, 43–44
Bankruptcy, filing, 38
Baseline budget, creation, 111
Bear market, defining, 181
Benchmark, measurement, 180
Beneficiary information
  placement, 287
  update, 289
Bill payments
  account, usage, 43
  timeliness, 56
Bond
  defining, 178
  fund, 179
Boss of My Money (podcast), 106
Boutin, Melisa, 146–148, 152
Brand-name products, money leaks, 98
Brokerage
  commissions, 194
  firm, function, 178

Budget
alignment, spending habits (adjustments/ sacrifice), 107–108
basis, 86
breakdown, 87–88
creation, 86, 289
fun money designation, 103
student loan payments, factoring, 150
Budgeting
avoidance, fear, 102
basics, 85–87
challenges, 100–102
consistency, challenging, 102
initiation, motivation, 106–107
learning, 241
low income, usage, 113–115
percentage breakdown, 91–93
plan, implementation (challenges/ setbacks), 109
practice, 87
styles, 90–95
usage, 111–112
Budget-naming skills, 85
Buffett, Warren, 57
Bull market, defining, 181
Business
budget
control, 269–270
worksheet, 296
finances, management, 250
Buy Now, Pay Later (BNPL), 134–136

C

Cable TV, cutting, 157
Capital gains, 180
Career
advancement, 263–264
aspirations, goals (alignment), 261–262
growth, 260–261
Carpooling, usage, 158
Cashback credit cards
rewards credit cards, contrast, 162–163
usage, 163
Cash-back rewards, earning, 38–39
Cash flow
increase, prioritization, 37–38
tracking, 269–270
Cash system, usage, 932
Cash value insurance (universal/whole life), 235
Cellphone plan, reduction, 158
Change, approach, 17
Children
activities/outings, cost, 88–89
budget creation, 88–89
needs, budget accounting, 288

Circle of influence,
shift, 32–36
Compensation strategy,
256–259
Compounding, function,
174–175
Conscious consumerism,
focus, 248
Core values, defining, 73–74
Couple budgeting, 115–118
Couples budgeting
listening/communication,
importance, 117
plan, 117
Credit
applications, avoidance,
215–216
bad credit score, rebuilding
problem (myth), 220
basics, 207–209
checking, 221
education, motivation,
225–226
example, 223–227
freezing, value, 217–218,
221–222
history
length, 209
record, 207
inquiries, 210
maintenance, 214–217, 226
mix, 209
monitoring service,
usage, 220
myths, 218–220
payment history, 209
rebuilding, 214–217
repair companies, value
(examination), 217
report, copy
(obtaining), 214
standing, education (motivation), 225–226
usage, advice, 208–209
utilization, 209
Credit Card Accountability
Responsibility and
Disclosure Act
(2009), 134
Credit cards
abuse, 38
accounts, continuation, 216
balance, continuation
(myth), 219
debt, impact, 224
destruction, 138
interest, money leaks, 98
unused cards, closing
(myth), 219
usage, 130
Credit scores, 209–218
cell phone bill payment,
impact (myth),
218–219
checking, myth, 219–220
factors, 209–213
improvement, 213–214
report, checking, 213–217

D
Debt
avalanche method, 141–143
avoidance, 80
challenges/setbacks, facing/overcoming, 64–65
consolidation, 143–144, 155–156
disappearance, 79
excess, 135
fear, money leaks, 101
freedom, journey, 79
payoff plan, creation, 226–227, 287
problems, 133
reduction, 137–138, 215
repayment
acceleration, 160–161
strategy, creation, 138
savings, 122
snowball method, 139–141
visual representation, importance, 137–138
"Debt is normal" mentality, 33
Debt payment, 6, 64, 69, 78–79, 160
advice, 161
challenges, 226
frame of mind, 166–168
goals, 164–166
ideas, 155–159
plan/strategy, 89, 139–144, 240
Demotivation, feeling, 35
Dependent information, update, 290
Digital detox, 280–281
Diversification, meaning, 178
Dividend, profit share, 180
Dreams
identification, 27–28
importance, 28

E
Economic cycles, 177
Economic developments, attention, 201
Embarrassment, negative emotion, 22
Emergency funds
adequacy, 288
creation, 138
money supply, 87–88
setup, 286
usage, 56
Emergency savings, 121–124
access, 123
account, usage, 43
building, 240
funding process, 122–123
need, quantity, 121–122
Emotional decisions, making, 258
Emotions
balance, 19–20
maintenance, 20
Employer
401(k) plan, 186–187, 225
contributions, 127

403(b) plan/457(b) plan, 186–187
investment plans, 187–188
matching, 189
Entrepreneurs, financial considerations, 272–273
Envelope system, usage, 93
Excessiveness, guilt (battle), 15
Exchange-traded fund (ETFs), index funds (comparison), 179
Expense ratio, 180
Expenses
control, 127–128
payment, 86
prioritization, 108, 111
reduction, 69
tracking, 113–114

F

Fair Isaac Corporation (FICO) score, 210–212
determination, process, 211–212
industry-specific FICO scores, 211
model, updates, 210–211
Fear, negative emotion, 20–21
Federal Student Aid (FAFSA), approach, 154
Female entrepreneurs, challenges, 273–274
Finances
control, 216–217
facing, 78
indecisiveness, 100
lack mentality, impact, 24–25
management, 249–250
navigation, advice, 250
ordering, 6
punishment, myth, 60–61
positive progress, prevention, 13
recession-proofing, 239–242
success, 8
transformation, success, 109
Financial actions, 287–289
Financial advisor
certifications/credentials, 196
communication, 196–197
fee type, 196
investment philosophy, 197
need, determination, 195–197
trust, 196
Financial behaviors, myth (influence), 58
Financial challenges, facing, 168–169
Financial confidence, increase, 241
Financial decisions, approach, 248
Financial goals, 75–77, 88

Financial goals (*Continued*)
achievement, 260–261, 264–265
circle of influence, impact, 32–33
review, 69
setting, 73
Financial journey, emotions (involvement), 19
Financial objectives, goals (alignment), 261–262
Financial plans, steps, 286–291
Financial records, control/tracking, 44–45
Financial security, 74
feeling, 184–185
Financial stability, maintenance (advice/strategies), 248–249
Financial success
achievement, 6
budget, usage, 85
motivation, 184
Financial wellness, 279–284
First-generation investor, challenges/overcoming/advice, 198–199, 201
First-generation wealth, building, 224–225
Food
money leaks, 97
quality, 281
Free money, offers, 133
Free rewards, 104
Friends/family, connection, 279
Funds, investment, 194
Fun money, designation, 103
Future
planning, 112
saving, 152
Future self, money supply, 87–88

G

Goals
achievement, 34–35, 264–265
clarity, 28
consideration, 7
creation, 261–262
impact, 18–19
setting, 75–77
Graduate school, completion (challenges), 147
Gratitude, practice, 281–282, 288–289
Groceries
money leaks, 97
spending, reduction, 158–159

H

Habits. *See* Bad money habits
addressing, 64
breaking, difficulty, 55
Happiness, clarity, 6–7
Health insurance, 232

Home-based business/home office, insuring, 233–234
Home burglary, protection, 234
Homeowner's insurance, 233–234
Household income, reduction (circumstances), 106
Housing, costs, 90

I
Identity theft, 218
  victimization, action, 222–223
Impulse shopping, budgeting challenges, 101
Income
  inconsistency, budgeting (usage), 111–112
  increase, 69, 112
  streams, creation, 241–242
Index funds, 179
  investment options, 59
Influence. *See* Circle of influence
Influencers, impact, 136–137
Information, compromise, 221–223
Insurance
  options, review, 287
  records, organization/tracking, 45
  types, 232–236
  update, 288
  usage, 231–237
Internet, usefulness, 35
Investing
  basics, 173–182
  concepts, 175–182
  defining/importance, 173–174
  initiation, 192–197
  learning, 15
Investment
  diversification, 240–241
  failures/setbacks, experience, 200–201
  inheritance, tax implications, 289
  money need, myth, 58–59
  objectives, 175–176
  plans, benefits/drawbacks, 187–189
  success story, 199–200

J
Jealousy, negative emotion, 22–23
Job
  compensation strategy, 256–259
  contributions, payment assumptions, 257–258
  exit, fear (avoidance), 259
  negotiation, 253–259
  unique/valuable abilities, leveraging, 255

Job (*Continued*)
- value, demonstration, 262–263

Joint accounts, closure, 289

L

Lack mentality
- defining, 23–24
- existence/overcoming, personal experience (impact), 24
- impact, 24–25
- shift, 25

Layaway plan, usage, 135
Liabilities, subtraction, 67
Life
- change, debt freedom (impact), 161–162
- goals, 88
- initiation, 6
- insurance, 234–235
- roles, balancing, 249
- stages/experiences, navigation, 8–9

Loan principle, payments (application), 161
Long-term disability insurance, 235
Long-term goals, 76, 117
Long-term investments
- acquisition, 69
- goals, 201–202

Long-term wealth, building, 74
Louie, Monica, 164–169
Low income, budgeting, 113–115
Low-Income Home Energy Assistance Program (LIHEAP), 114

M

Management fees, 194
Market trends, attention, 201
May, Steph, 259–265
McElroy, Naseema, 160–162
Memberships/subscriptions, cancellation, 159
Mental well-being, management, 290
Me-time, 104
Me Time, scheduling, 282
Mid-term goals, 76
Million-Dollar Game, 74
Mindfulness, practice, 281
Mindset
- adjustment, steps, 260–261
- impact, 6, 79
- positive mindset, lmaintenance, 263

Mistakes. *See* Money
- acknowledgment, 17
- occurrence, 9, 17

Money
- bad money habits, 55–61
- control, 50
- discussion
  - discomfort, 258
  - impoliteness, myth, 59–60
- emotions, relationship, 79

evil, root (myth), 58
freedom, advice, 71
goals, time allotment, 100
habits. *See* Bad money habits.
description, 62–63
improvement, 65
impact, 7, 19
leaks, attention, 96–99
mindset, development, 155
mistakes, 37–38
release, 13–18
myths, 58–61, 63
need. *See* Investment.
partner discussion, 287
relationship, change, 71
slipups, 13
tracking, 50
Monthly budget, creation, 56
Monthly money conversation, planning, 116
Motivation
clarity, 6–7
initiation, 18
Mutual fund, money pool, 178–179
Mychas, Christina, 62–65

N

Needs, prioritization, 114
Negative net worth, usage, 68
Networking, importance, 263–264
Net worth
building, 182–183
calculation, 67–68
increase, 69–71
knowledge, 67–70
Nonretirement investment accounts, usage, 43, 187
Nonretirement/nonemergency savings, usage, 156
Nunez, Mabel, 197–202

O

Omole, Adeola, 182–185
Overspending, 56

P

Part-time job, usage, 157
Passwords/PINs, changes, 222
Paycheck-to-paycheck cycle, repetition, 107
Percentage breakdown, 91–93
Permanent records, organization, 46
Perotte, Chavonne, 23–25
Personal article insurance, 235–236
Personal budget spreadsheet (Excel, usage), 293–294
Personal experience, impact, 24
Personal finance(s)
difficulty, myth, 59–60
management strategies, 250
self-care, relationship, 279–280
Personal growth, skills (development/improvement), 7

Peterson-KFF Health System Tracker, usage, 232
Pet insurance, 236
Physical health, prioritization, 288
Plan, adherence, 5
Portfolio, rebalancing, 195
Positive mindset, maintenance, 263
Positive money mindset, emotional balance, 18–23
Possession excess, sale, 157
Price comparisons, money leaks, 98
Promotion, achievement, 264–265
Prospectus, examination, 178

R

Raise/salary
  increase, 262
    achievement, 264–265
  negotiation, 253–259
  request, 254
    business transaction, 255
    research, 255–256
Rate of return (RoR), 176
Real estate investment trust (REIT), 59, 181
Recession-proof businesses, ideas, 245–247
Recession-proof jobs/businesses, 242–247
Recession-proof jobs, ideas, 242–245
Records
  keeping, duration, 45–47
  ordering, 43–47
Regret, negative emotion, 21
Relationships
  benefits, eligibility, 287
  building, 263–264
  lack mentality, impact, 24–25
Rental assistance, 114–115
Renter's insurance, 233
Retirement
  amount, requirement, 191–192
  concepts, 189–190
  early withdrawals, impact, 190
  fees, understanding, 193–194
  investing, 185–192
  investment accounts, usage, 43
  long-term investment, 193
  saving
    importance, 286
    location, 186–187
    rollover, 287–288
Retirement plan
  investment options, 189
  rollovers, 190
Retirement savings
  contribution, 127
  investment, 89–90
Reverse budgeting, 94
Rewards credit cards, usage, 163

Risk
  profile, 177
  tolerance, 176–177
    determination, 194
Roache, Lucille, 271–275
Robo-advisor, function, 178
Roth IRA, 187, 225

S

Salary. *See* Raise/salary
Sang, Ashlee, 247–250
Save yourself fund, 121–124
Savings, 105
  building, 130
  focus, 128
  reduction, 14–15
  story, 126–127
Scholarships, exploration, 153–154
Scott, Latoya, 37–39
Self-care
  nurturing, 279–284
  personal finances, relationship, 279–280
  practices, 280–282
Self-forgiveness, 16–17
Self-negotiation, 56
Self-reward, 102–105
Shame, negative emotion, 22
Shopping addiction, money habits (impact), 62–63
Short-term goals, 75–76
Side hustles, 265–271
  business budget, 269–270
  cash flow, tracking, 269–270
  client identification/ attraction, strategies, 272
  female entrepreneurs, challenges, 273–274
  financial considerations, 272–273
  full-time work, combination, 273
  ideas, 266–270
  initiation, 129, 157
  moneymaking, goal, 268
  operating expenses, 269
  plan, clarity, 268
  profits, assessment, 269–270
  recurring income, generation, 271–272
  startup costs, 269
Sinking funds
  building, 126
  emergency savings, contrast, 125
  number, determination, 125
  usage, 124–126
Sleep, obtaining (importance), 282
Spending
  habits, addressing, 64
  habits, adjustments/sacrifice (budget alignment), 108
  hiding, 13–14
  journal, review, 52
  tracking, 50–52
Splurging, occurrence, 13–14
Startup expenses, 295

Stillman, Molly, 78–80
Stock
  investment, 15–16, 178, 194
  market investor,
    journey, 198
Stress, management, 288
Student loans
  accountability buddy,
    usage, 159
  advice, 148
  approach, 148–154
  debt, 146–148
  facts/basics, 145–146
  forgiveness programs/
    employee benefit
    programs, 151–152
  payments
    automation, 159
    prioritization, 151
    skipping, avoidance, 151
  terms/conditions,
    awareness, 149–150
Subscriptions,
    money leaks, 97
Success, money (impact), 39
Supplemental Nutrition
    Assistance program
    (SNAP), 114
Support system/community,
    presence, 288
Suttle, Brittney, 70–71

T

Target date fund, 179
Tax
  joint tax plan,
    placement, 287
  payments/brackets,
    consideration, 188–189
  refunds/bonuses, usage, 159
Term life insurance, 234–235
Traditional IRA, 186
Transactions, tracking, 86

U

Universal life insurance, 235
Unnecessary costs, cutting,
    113–114

V

Values, defining, 73–74
VantageScore, 212–213
Virtual mentors, usage, 35
Volatility, impact, 180
Voogd, Peter, 32

W

Wealth, building, 226–227
Wealthy, affirmation, 27
Whole life insurance, 235
"Woe is me" emotions, 35
Work
  promotion, advice, 265
  value, demonstra-
    tion, 262–263

Y

Yield, impact, 180

Z

Zennial, credit example,
    223–227